C000151590

OSCAR WILDE

OSCAR WILDE

Selected Poems

Edited with an Introduction by
Malcolm Hicks

Fyfield*Books*

First published in 1992 by
Carcanet Press Limited
208-212 Corn Exchange Buildings
Manchester M4 3BQ

Selection and introduction copyright © 1992 Malcolm Hicks
The right of Malcolm Hicks to be identified as the editor of
this work has been asserted by him in accordance
with the Copyright, Designs and Patents Act of 1988.
All rights reserved

A CIP catalogue record for this book is
available from the British Library.
ISBN 0 85635 984 X

The publisher acknowledges financial assistance from
the Arts Council of Great Britain

Set in 10pt Palatino by Bryan Williamson, Darwen
Printed and bound in England by SRP Ltd, Exeter

Contents

Introduction

When Oscar Wilde's only collection of poems was first published in the summer of 1881, critical scythes were whetted and waiting. The twenty-six year-old *arriviste*, who had been so flamboyantly advertising himself as both prophet and practiser of an aesthetic renaissance, could hardly expect a sympathetic press for what appeared to be the overdue fruits of his genius.[1] Reviewers, imbued with large measures of Victorian high-mindedness, were on their mettle to prune the extravagance. In the late 1870s, having gained a rare double first, Wilde had come down from Oxford where he had conspicuously 'created himself' in living out a variety of cultural impulses, in exploring the interrelationships between life, art, and artifice.[2] He sought to announce his presence in London, and proved remarkably successful in doing so. Bringing to mind the Wildean witticism that there is only one thing worse than being talked about, and that is *not* being talked about, we might cite the production of Gilbert and Sullivan's *Patience* in April 1881, which launched D'Oyly Carte's new venue, the Savoy Theatre. The amusingly satirical treatment of *Patience*'s duo of aesthetes, the ethereal Grosvenor and the fleshly Bunthorne, was largely a response to the phenomenon of Oscar Fingal O'Flahertie Wills Wilde. This helped to set the stage (so to speak) for the advent of the *Poems* some two months later. 'What has he done, this young man, that one meets him everywhere? Oh yes he talks well, but what has he done? He has written nothing, he does not paint or act – he does nothing but talk. I do not understand.' Thus queried the celebrated Polish actress, Helen Modjeska,[3] who had arrived in London in 1880 to play in an adaptation of Dumas' *La Dame aux Camélias* (and who, before long, succumbed to the charm and became a good friend of this same young man). What he had done, and was doing, was soon to be before the public gaze.

Reactions to the *Poems* were at best mixed, or unfavourable. Negative critical opinion is summed up in the influential *Saturday Review*'s comment that the volume is 'marred everywhere by imitation [and] insincerity . . .'. The consensus on the positive side acknowledges what the same periodical calls an 'astonishing fluency' (an unsettling analogue, perhaps, of the so-called insincere), or what the Chicago *Dial* echoed as poetry 'striking in form and treatment, and polished in workmanship...'. Unappreciative of Wilde's complex evocations of past masters, of his dissolution of crude distinctions between life and art and his promulgation of newly synthesized truths and beauty, what Matthew Arnold had identified as the severely 'Hebraic' age concluded that expressive powers were wasted. 'Nothing to say', complained the *Saturday Review*; no 'distinct message' the *Athenaeum*. One could multiply the refinements, the contrasts – 'virility and freedom' *vis-à-vis* unmanliness, or sensuousness lacking purpose – but the general outlines are clear enough.[4]

Despite our own century's proliferation of critical discriminations, which might well be thought to promise sympathetic revisions of judgement, Wilde's poetic reputation remains largely unsung, or sung with a few discordant notes that little advance the strain of his contemporaries. After all, Wilde the man, who suggested he put his genius (and its attendant provocations) into his life, and only his talent into his art, has gone, and we might look for subtle reappraisals of this equally subtle disclaimer from those no longer challenged by his presence. The critical inheritance, however, perpetuates the assumed imbalance. The life has been exhaustively rehearsed, and requires only occasional mention here; but where Wilde the poet – as distinct from dramatist, essayist, and fiction writer – does manage to get attention, a critical malaise is manifest.

In a review of Wilde's letters first published in 1963, W.H. Auden, exploits the discrepancy between the life and the art to suggest that none of Wilde's writing is much worth attending to; the poetry, above all, being still-born:

> It is impossible for us to be just to Wilde because, although his contemporaries all agreed that his improvised conversation was superior to his writings, they also thought the latter much better than we do. Of his poems not one has survived, for he was totally lacking in a poetic voice of his own; what he wrote was an imitation of poetry-in-general.[5]

8

Auden's dismissiveness rehashes those jibes of imitation and insincerity of Wilde's own generation. His comments resurface in a collection of critical essays published in 1969, edited by the writer of the possibly definitive biography of Wilde, the sympathetic Richard Ellmann. Significantly these 'Twentieth Century Views' scarcely notice the poetry, and are of a somewhat vintage status – one of them retrieved from the writings of one of Wilde's earliest mentors while still at Oxford, the nineteenth-century scholar and aesthete, Walter Pater. A book of 'Modern Critical Views', published as late as 1985, continues the general impasse, with Wilde the poet briefly discounted in an introduction to a collection of essays which includes extensive regurgitations of material to be found in Ellmann's edition.[6]

Modern society is avowedly free from prejudice and taboo; but, at least where the earlier slightings of Wilde's poetic art are concerned, one does wonder if the legacy of Wilde's sexual notoriety still lingers – however obliquely, or even unwittingly. The bulk of the poetry was composed some time before Wilde engaged in any overt homosexual practice (there are fine poems on heterosexual romance and passionate recall); but the novelist and critic, George Moore, for example, writing – long after the scandal had settled – to Wilde's old companion, Frank Harris, uncharitably highlights the paradoxes of both a life and an art where one distasteful and damning accusation is seen to be the deciding factor for both subsequent fame and subsequent disregard:

> ... I do not think that anybody would have troubled about him if the Marquis of Queensbury had not written him a postcard; had it not been for that unlucky postcard Wilde and his literature would be sleeping comfortably in the dust at the bottom of an almost forgotten drawer...[7]

The cleverly ambiguous reference to 'that unlucky postcard' alludes, of course, to Lord Alfred Douglas's father's insinuations of sodomy on Wilde's part (which, ironically enough, were probably misinformed), Wilde's action of libel and Queensbury's acquittal, followed by Wilde's own arrest and trials for perjury, resulting in a sentence of two years' hard labour, 1895-97.[8]

Imprisonment did at least engender *The Ballad of Reading Gaol*, the last work of what proved to be a broken man. First published in 1898, some two years before Wilde's death, this substantial and impressive poem was considerably praised for its sincerity, allied to moral and imaginative power. This perceived combination of qualities has secured it as the sole surviving emblem of Wilde's poetic reputation. A generation before Auden's strictures, the popular 'Everyman's Library' included the *Ballad* – and only the *Ballad* – in its first publication of a selected *Plays, Prose Writings and Poems [sic]*. A generation after Auden, the volume has been reprinted (1991) and under Professor Terry Eagleton's aegis the *Ballad* is still the only poem to be included.

Wilde felt sufficiently confident about the quality of his first collection of poems to send copies for approval to Browning, Arnold and Swinburne, among others; and, as one of the 'poet[s] ... of England', proudly defended his 'imaginative and beautiful work' when a complimentary copy was rejected by students of the Oxford Union.[9] The poems' preoccupations remain vital, exploring the interrelationship, the symbiosis, that exists between life and an intensely felt art in a world which seems to have lost its vision. Wilde's contemporaries were temperamentally disinclined to discover in the poetry's ample illustration of these cross-fertilizations the 'message' they wanted. It is surely his purpose, in his eclectic evocations of 'Hellenism', interwoven with a decidedly English countryside, to reinvigorate the Arnoldian ideal of 'sweetness and light' in the face of that perdurable and pervasive philistinism which Arnold himself had so tellingly analysed in his *Culture and Anarchy* essays of 1869. Attractively Oxonian in both cultural and geographic provenance, a number of the longer poems originate from the brilliant young Classicist's vagrant musings in the Oxfordshire countryside. Throughout Wilde's poetry the appreciation of transient beauty – delicately, meditatively realized in the 'Impressions', for example – poeticizes the poignant evocation of the momentary enshrined in Pater's *Renaissance* (1873) – particularly its infamous 'Conclusion' – as much as it suggests French example. But too much sleuth-hunting for precursors has clouded criticism of several of Wilde's writings, and reflects the bald censure of the poetry for being second-hand and insincere. Equally, the accumulation of sensuous imagery and its echoes has given rise to allied matters of taste. In 1910 one American Professor of Languages was led to reflect that 'to read [Wilde's] verse at all is cloying, and to read much of it is like a literary debauch'; yet he did generously concede the fluency: 'no minor poet in England ever attained a more thorough mastery of technique'.[10] The division between form and content is curious: the ingenuity of style suffuses the richness of the subject matter, and it is tempting to assume that Wilde's mastery of manner was the poetic complement of his arresting powers of speech and conversation.

Wilde's own sophisticated prose implicitly pours scorn on anyone who might task his poetry for being artificial. Life and art are a complex amalgam; life is, indeed, 'textual'. The dialogue form that Wilde favoured multiplies the free play of his own mind as his brilliant dialecticians refract the light from other minds in their versatile dissolution of boundaries between fact and fiction. At one impassioned moment in *The Critic as Artist*, Gilbert, having rehearsed, re-imagined, 'rewritten', and thus renewed the *Iliad* of Homer, bursts forth: 'Shadows in a song? No, they are real. Action! What is action? It dies at the moment of its energy. It is a base concession to fact. The world is made by the singer for the dreamer.' Ernest replies: 'While you talk it seems to me to be so.' To which Gilbert rejoins: 'It is so in truth...'. The 'religious' earnestness expressed here, together with Gilbert's 'conversion' is a challenge to the earnestness of a Victorian reading (and theatre-going) public hamstrung by its insistence on clear-cut distinctions between fact and fiction, on a fiction in the service of fact as a summons to action, with a critical vocabulary of terms like 'insincerity', 'imitation', or 'plagiarism' reserved for any poet who sought for life in the redefinition of earlier writing. 'Age will mellow down his muse,' the sympathetic Walter Hamilton reassured the public in 1882 when, in his book, *The Aesthetic Movement in England*, he looked forward to much more from Wilde the poet.[11] This was not to be; and it is possible to read much of the later prose writing as an oblique defence of his poetic practice which, after 1881, he revived only in the arrestingly elusive 'Harlot's House', the outrageous *Sphinx*, and, at the last, the chastened *Ballad of Reading Gaol*.

It could be argued that Wilde readily indulged in aesthetic pro-selytizing precisely because he knew it was likely to fall on deaf or disagreeing ears. Yet in both his art and the generous examples of his life, his insistent rejection of moral severity and moral realism nourish the Arnoldian (in Wilde's terms often the truly Christian) desire both to humanize and civilize. In *The Decay of Lying*, completed in December 1888, Vivian exclaims: 'We have mistaken the common livery of the age for the vesture of the Muses, and spend our days in the sordid streets and hideous suburbs of our vile cities when we should be out on the hillside with Apollo.' The *Poems* do much to encourage Apollonian encounters, but the poetical climate was scarcely encouraging. Of the Victorian triumvirate, Arnold had long since renounced his poetry for its failure consistently to 'animate', for 'at best [its awakening] a pleasing melancholy.' Tennyson's preservation of some Wordsworthian visionary gleams translated into Christian yea-saying had made its impact and had gone. Browning, at least as acutely aware as Wilde himself of the naïvety of distinctions between fact and fancy, was engaged in lengthy poetic ratiocinations on the subject in the face of erosion of Biblical 'truths', which were as little understood in his own day as they are in ours. And had Wilde arrived at Oxford some years earlier, to say nothing of his distaste for the mob, he would scarcely have joined those who chanted Swinburne's 'Hymn to Proserpine' down the High. 'Thou has conquered, O pale Galilean; the world has grown grey from thy breath' – published in *Poems and Ballads* (1866), with its tart historical lament for the last vestiges of Hellenism, it was not the voice to be followed, beyond occasional Swinburnian atmospherics, by a youthful Wilde still debating what mode of faith might witness Christ's essential humanity. 'Charmides', in fact, which Wilde thought the best of the *Poems*, is a rich and strange tale of the triumph of love in death in the face of classical deities, who are at least as severe in judgement as any withering blast of Christian law.

In the face of the vast symbolic landscape of Egdon Heath at the beginning of *The Return of the Native*, published some three years before Wilde's *Poems*, Thomas Hardy had surmised that 'the new Vale of Tempe may be a gaunt waste in Thule'. Wilde

determined to seek the inspiriting Vale of Tempe on English soil
– that beautiful Vale in Thessaly, celebrated by Greek and Latin
poets. His poetry testifies rapturously to nature and the presence
of the Gods alive in an ambience created out of his love for his
cherished English forbears. And yet there is a sense of loss, of
belatedness. Rodney Shewan astutely observes that 'the volume
[of Wilde's *Poems*] reads like a personal anthology through which
the poet, as nostalgic critic of some five centuries of verse,
attempts to define his relationship to a tradition which has disin-
tegrated before he has had the chance to contribute to it.'[12] Yet
Wilde is above pastiche, and the debate with tradition must be
seen in a wider context. The young poet (like the older essayist)
is as committed to the world as he is to books, which the poetry
'attempts to define' in accomplished remodellings of past masters' (and mistresses) voices as they range that world. Milton (via
Wordsworth) is summoned in sonnets on contemporary religious
and political issues; Browning is glimpsed at in the romantic
monologue; Keats, Spenser, Arnold, Shakespeare reverberate in
the longer pastorals; the *Ballad* owes something to Coleridge
(something, perhaps, to the younger A.E. Housman); *The Sphinx*
remembers Poe... 'Plagiarism' might be the cry of some contemporaries (akin to Auden's 'imitation of poetry-in-general'), yet
the plagiarist is one who borrows ideas or language without
assimilating them to his own purpose and transmuting them by
his own personality. The poems are woven by a vastly resourceful
sensibility where the resultant tapestry is distinctly Wilde's own.
For a writer who never tired of elaborating, brilliantly, an acute
sense of the way art informs life (and *vice versa*) to demand some
curiously prisine poetic artefact would, rightly, be dismissed as
commonplace, if not impossible.

Let me allude to Wilde's expansive vision with one limiting
illustration. Meditating (on William Morris's own 'rewriting' of
Chaucer and Spenser) on a midsummer excursion within the
recesses of an Oxford wood, what civilized mind might not reflect
(via Matthew Arnold) on even greater masters? What Wilde's
mind delightfully 'interleaves' is a living echo of the pastoral
scenes of Shakespeare's *Winter's Tale*. The lines can be innocently
enjoyed, yet they offer a vital modification of sensibility to the

13

'literary' reader, rather than a dryasdust catalogue of writerly bits and pieces:

> Far from the cricket-ground and noisy eight,
>   At Bagley, where the rustling bluebells come
> Almost before the blackbird finds a mate
>   And overstay the swallow, and the hum
> Of many murmuring bees flits through the leaves,
> Have I lain poring on the dreamy tales his fancy weaves,...
>   'The Garden of Eros,' ll.175-80

If, where the personal voice is raised in the *Poems*, there is a sense of posturing, they are not necessarily the worse for it. The relish or rejection of apparent artifice looks to be a matter of taste; and Wilde's sonnets addressed to actor-friends, subsumed into their roles as protagonists, comment astutely on the paradox of life made more real by the theatrical. 'Camma', a sonnet addressed to Ellen Terry who played the part of Camma in Tennyson's *The Cup*, fervently spotlights and complicates the issue at its close by invoking Antony and Cleopatra: 'I am grown sick of unreal passions, make / The world thine Actium, me thine Antony!' In Wilde's novel, *The Picture of Dorian Grey* (1890-91), Sibyl Vane lives the parts she plays; *qua* Sibyl Vane, Dorian (cruelly) considers her nothing. In this work the exuberance of artifice is cumulatively troubled by the mirror image of despair. Yet, in the *Poems*, where self-definition is so successfully sustained in the creative embrace of 'intertextuality', the problem rarely surfaces. The impression of freshness – the combination of rich, surprising imagery with Wilde's absolute mastery of fluid form, fluid argument – obliterates any sense of stale or stagnant echo.

How does the writer create a space of his or her own in the face of the exhaustive achievements of predecessors – the 'burden of the precursor', as the dilemma is known and complexly debated on in modern literary scholarship? The burden looks to be a boon where Wilde is concerned: his *doppelgänger* paradoxically proving to be the inspiriting wraith of past masters' presences. 'Make it new,' Ezra Pound demanded in the ringing title he chose for a volume of essays in the early 1900s. Yet as late as 1922, after four hundred lines of verse which sardonically evoke a lost literary past in order to chastise a barren present, the con-cluding voice of T.S. Eliot's *The Waste Land* speaks fragilely of 'these fragments [that] I have shored against my ruins'. One can-not turn Wilde into a proto-Modernist, but it is arresting to find how Shewan's remarks, previously quoted (p.13), might possibly be applied to T.S. Eliot. Wilde's position does seem to prelude the impasse out of which a distinctively modernist expression was forged a generation or more later. His poems vitalize the past as a renaissance in the present, which he was uniquely fitted so to do – not the twilight that his critical detractors maintain, but a glorious sunset. It is time they were appreciated.

Notes

1   A small number of shorter poems, and a goodly number of fugitive prose pieces, had already appeared in various periodicals. The poems were mostly revised for book publication. *Ravenna*, Wilde's Newdigate Prize Poem at Oxford had been published in 1878. His first play, *Vera; or, The Nihilists* had circulated in a privately printed form dating from the previous year to the *Poems*. As early as 1914 only two copies of this edition of *Vera* were known. See Stuart Mason, *Bibliography of Oscar Wilde* (London: T. Werner Laurie Ltd., [1914]), particularly p.249.

2   See, for example, Richard Ellmann, *Oscar Wilde* (Penguin Books, [1988]), p.95, and *passim*. First published, 1987.

3   Most recently quoted by Ellmann: *Oscar Wilde*, p.112.

4   A selection of contemporary and near contemporary responses are usefully gathered in Karl Beckson, ed., *Oscar Wilde: The Critical Heritage* (London: Routledge & Kegan Paul, [1970]), pp.33-54.

5   See 'An Improbable Life' in Richard Ellmann, ed., *Oscar Wilde: A Collection of Critical Essays*, (N.J.: Prentice-Hall, Inc., [1969]), p.134.

6   See Harold Bloom, ed., *Oscar Wilde: Modern Critical Views* (New York: Chelsea House, 1985), p.1.

7   *Oscar Wilde: The Critical Heritage*, p.385.

8   For the details here it is best to consult Ellmann's *Oscar Wilde*.

9   Ibid., pp.137-41.

10   *Oscar Wilde: The Critical Heritage*, p.318.

11   A useful excerpt is to be found in *Oscar Wilde: The Critical Heritage*, pp.48-49.

12   *Oscar Wilde: Art and Egotism* ([London]: Macmillan, [1977]), p.9.

Suggestions for further reading

Prose Writings and Letters

No annotated edition of the complete works exists. *The First Collected Edition of the Works of Oscar Wilde*, 15 vols., edited by Robert Ross and first published by Methuen & Co. (1908), is comprehensive. It was reprinted in 1969 by Dawsons of Pall Mall.

Rupert Hart-Davis, ed., *The Letters of Oscar Wilde* (London: [Rupert Hart-Davis Ltd.], 1962).

Rupert Hart-Davis, ed., *More Letters of Oscar Wilde* ([London]: John Murray, [1985]).

Bibliographies

Stuart Mason, *Bibliography of Oscar Wilde*, with a note by Robert Ross (London: T. Werner Laurie Ltd., [1914]).

E.K. Mikhail, *Oscar Wilde: An Annotated Bibliography of Criticism* ([London]: Macmillan, [1978]).

Biography and Criticism

Biographies and memoirs are legion, mostly informative but duplicating details. The latest is recommended:

Richard Ellmann, *Oscar Wilde* (Penguin Books, [1988]), first published 1987.

Edouard Roditi, *Oscar Wilde* (Norfolk, Connecticut: New Directions Books, [1947]).

Richard Ellmann, ed., *Oscar Wilde: A Collection of Critical Essays* (N.J.: Prentice-Hall, Inc., [1969]).

Karl Beckson, ed., *Oscar Wilde: The Critical Heritage* (London: Routledge & Kegan Paul, [1970]).

Rodney Shewan, *Oscar Wilde: Art and Egotism* ([London]: Macmillan, [1977]).

A Note on the Text *(Editions of Wilde's Poems)*

The first edition of the *Poems* appeared in June 1881. It comprises a modest number of poems, with revisions, which had been previously published in various periodicals, together with a substantial number of works making their first appearance. The edition consisted of two hundred and fifty copies of a printing of seven hundred and fifty; the remaining five hundred making up what were called the second and third editions, which appeared within the year. The fourth and fifth editions of 1882 also derived from one printing, and incorporated a small number of alterations of substance. The 'Author's Edition', ten years later, was made up of copies of the fifth edition.

In 1908 the first collected edition of Wilde's works appeared under the general editorship of Wilde's old friend, and *confidant*, Robert Ross. The *Poems* (Vol. IX) follows the fourth edition, yet restores two stanzas of 'Charmides' which were cancelled in the 1892 editions. It also adds *Ravenna*, the Newdigate Prize Poem from the edition of 1878, Wilde's translations, and important uncollected poems (including 'The Harlot's House', *The Sphinx*, and *The Ballad of Reading Gaol*).

The present selection is based upon the poetry volume of this first collected edition. It follows the arrangements of that edition, which in turn follows that of the earlier editions, with the uncollected works and translations following after. The only exception is the placing of passages from *Ravenna* later in the selection, to enable 'Hélas!' to make its introductory impact as Wilde intended (see 'Notes on the Poems'). For the first time line numbers have been added to the longer poems for ease of reference.

Hélas!

To drift with every passion till my soul
Is a stringed lute on which all winds can play,
Is it for this that I have given away
Mine ancient wisdom, and austere control?
Methinks my life is a twice-written scroll
Scrawled over on some boyish holiday
With idle songs for pipe and virelay,
Which do but mar the secret of the whole.
Surely there was a time I might have trod
The sunlit heights, and from life's dissonance
Struck one clear chord to reach the ears of God:
Is that time dead? lo! with a little rod
I did but touch the honey of romance –
And must I lose a soul's inheritance?

Ave Imperatrix

Set in this stormy sea,
　Queen of these restless fields of tide,
England! what shall men say of thee,
　Before whose feet the worlds divide?

The earth, a brittle globe of glass,
　Lies in the hollow of thy hand,
And through its heart of crystal pass,
　Like shadows through a twilight land,

The spears of crimson-suited war,
　The long white-crested waves of fight,　　　　　10
And all the deadly fires which are
　The torches of the Lords of Night.

19

The yellow leopards, strained and lean,
    The treacherous Russian knows so well,
With gaping blackened jaws are seen
    Leap through the hail of screaming shell.

The strong sea-lion of England's wars
    Hath left his sapphire cave of sea,
To battle with the storm that mars
    The stars of England's chivalry.   20

The brazen-throated clarion blows
    Across the Pathan's reedy fen,
And the high steeps of Indian snows
    Shake to the tread of armèd men.

And many an Afghan chief, who lies
    Beneath his cool pomegranate-trees,
Clutches his sword in fierce surmise
    When on the mountain-side he sees

The fleet-foot Marri scout, who comes
    To tell how he hath heard afar   30
The measured roll of English drums
    Beat at the gates of Kandahar.

For southern wind and east wind meet
    Where, girt and crowned by sword and fire,
England with bare and bloody feet
    Climbs the steep road of wide empire.

O lonely Himalayan height,
    Grey pillar of the Indian sky,
Where saw'st thou last in clanging flight
    Our wingèd dogs of Victory!   40

The almond groves of Samarcand,
    Bokhara, where red lilies blow,
And Oxus, by whose yellow sand
    The grave white-turbaned merchants go:

And on from thence to Ispahan,
  The gilded garden of the sun,
Whence the long dusty caravan
  Brings cedar wood and vermilion;

And that dread city of Cabool
  Set at the mountain's scarpèd feet,   50
Whose marble tanks are ever full
  With water for the noonday heat:

Where through the narrow straight Bazaar
  A little maid Circassian
Is led, a present from the Czar
  Unto some old and bearded khan, –

Here have our wild war-eagles flown,
  And flapped wide wings in fiery fight;
But the sad dove, that sits alone
  In England – she hath no delight.   60

In vain the laughing girl will lean
  To greet her love with love-lit eyes:
Down in some treacherous black ravine,
  Clutching his flag, the dead boy lies.

And many a moon and sun will see
  The lingering wistful children wait
To climb upon their father's knee;
  And in each house made desolate

Pale women who have lost their lord
  Will kiss the relics of the slain –   70
Some tarnished epaulette – some sword –
  Poor toys to soothe such anguished pain.

For not in quiet English fields
  Are these, our brothers, lain to rest,
Where we might deck their broken shields
  With all the flowers the dead love best.

For some are by the Delhi walls,
    And many in the Afghan land,
And many where the Ganges falls
    Through seven mouths of shifting sand. 80

And some in Russian waters lie,
    And others in the seas which are
The portals to the East, or by
    The wind-swept heights of Trafalgar.

O wandering graves! O restless sleep!
    O silences of the sunless day!
O still ravine! O stormy deep!
    Give up your prey! Give up your prey!

And thou whose wounds are never healed,
    Whose weary race is never won, 90
O Cromwell's England! must thou yield
    For every inch of ground a son?

Go! crown with thorns thy gold-crowned head,
    Change thy glad song to song of pain;
Wind and wild wave have got thy dead,
    And will not yield them back again.

Wave and wild wind and foreign shore
    Possess the flower of English land –
Lips that thy lips shall kiss no more,
    Hands that shall never clasp thy hand. 100

What profit now that we have bound
    The whole round world with nets of gold,
If hidden in our heart is found
    The care that groweth never old?

What profit that our galleys ride,
    Pine-forest-like, on every main?
Ruin and wreck are at our side,
    Grim warders of the House of pain.

Where are the brave, the strong, the fleet?
    Where is our English chivalry?   110
Wild grasses are their burial-sheet,
    And sobbing waves their threnody.

O loved ones lying far away,
    What word of love can dead lips send!
O wasted dust! O senseless clay!
    Is this the end! is this the end!

Peace, peace! we wrong the noble dead
    To vex their solemn slumber so;
Though childless, and with thorn-crowned head,
    Up the steep road must England go,   120

Yet when this fiery web is spun,
    Her watchmen shall descry from far
The young Republic like a sun
    Rise from these crimson seas of war.

The Garden of Eros

It is full summer now, the heart of June,
    Not yet the sunburnt reapers are astir
Upon the upland meadow where too soon
    Rich autumn time, the season's usurer,
Will lend his hoarded gold to all the trees,
And see his treasure scattered by the wild and spendthrift
        breeze.

Too soon indeed! yet here the daffodil,
    That love-child of the Spring, has lingered on
To vex the rose with jealousy, and still
    The harebell spreads her azure pavilion,   10
And like a strayed and wandering reveller
Abandoned of its brothers, whom long since June's
        messenger

23

The missel-thrush has frighted from the glade,
    One pale narcissus loiters fearfully
Close to a shadowy nook, where half afraid
    Of their own loveliness some violets lie
That will not look the gold sun in the face
For fear of too much splendour, – ah! methinks it is a place

Which should be trodden by Persephone
    When wearied of the flowerless fields of Dis!   20
Or danced on by the lads of Arcady!
    The hidden secret of eternal bliss
Known to the Grecian here a man might find,
Ah! you and I may find it now if Love and Sleep be kind.

There are the flowers which mourning Herakles
    Strewed on the tomb of Hylas, columbine,
Its white doves all a-flutter where the breeze
    Kissed them too harshly, the small celandine,
That yellow-kirtled chorister of eve,
And lilac lady's-smock, – but let them bloom alone, and
        leave   30

Yon spirèd hollyhock red-crocketed
    To sway its silent chimes, else must the bee,
Its little bellringer, go seek instead
    Some other pleasaunce; the anemone
That weeps at daybreak, like a silly girl
Before her love, and hardly lets the butterflies unfurl

Their painted wings beside it, – bid it pine
    In pale virginity; the winter snow
Will suit it better than those lips of thine
    Whose fires would but scorch it, rather go   40
And pluck that amorous flower which blooms alone,
Fed by the pander wind with dust of kisses not its own.

The trumpet-mouths of red convolvulus
   So dear to maidens, creamy meadow-sweet
Whiter than Juno's throat and odorous
   As all Arabia, hyacinths the feet
Of Huntress Dian would be loth to mar
For any dappled fawn, – pluck these, and those fond
     flowers which are

Fairer than what Queen Venus trod upon
   Beneath the pines of Ida, eucharis,   50
That morning star which does not dread the sun,
   And budding marjoram which but to kiss
Would sweeten Cytheræa's lips and make
Adonis jealous, – these for thy head, – and for thy girdle take

Yon curving spray of purple clematis
   Whose gorgeous dye outflames the Tyrian King,
And foxgloves with their nodding chalices,
   But that one narciss which the startled Spring
Let from her kirtle fall when first she heard
In her own woods the wild tempestuous song of summer's
     bird,   60

Ah! leave it for a subtle memory
   Of those sweet tremulous days of rain and sun,
When April laughed between her tears to see
   The early primrose with shy footsteps run
From the gnarled oak-tree roots till all the wold,
Spite of its brown and trampled leaves, grew bright with
     shimmering gold.

Nay, pluck it too, it is not half so sweet
   As thou thyself, my soul's idolatry!
And when thou art a-wearied at thy feet
   Shall oxlips weave their brightest tapestry,   70
For thee the woodbine shall forget its pride
And veil its tangled whorls, and thou shalt walk on daisies
     pied.

And I will cut a reed by yonder spring
    And make the wood-gods jealous, and old Pan
Wonder what young intruder dares to sing
    In these still haunts, where never foot of man
Should tread at evening, lest he chance to spy
The marble limbs of Artemis and all her company.

And I will tell thee why the jacinth wears
    Such dread embroidery of dolorous moan,   80
And why the hapless nightingale forbears
    To sing her song at noon, but weeps alone
When the fleet swallow sleeps, and rich men feast,
And why the laurel trembles when she sees the lightening
        east.

And I will sing how sad Proserpina
    Unto a grave and gloomy Lord was wed,
And lure the silver-breasted Helena
    Back from the lotus meadows of the dead,
So shalt thou see that awful loveliness
For which two mighty Hosts met fearfully in war's abyss!   90

And then I'll pipe to thee that Grecian tale
    How Cynthia loves the lad Endymion,
And hidden in a grey and misty veil
    Hies to the cliffs of Latmos once the Sun
Leaps from his ocean bed in fruitless chase
Of those pale flying feet which fade away in his embrace.

And if my flute can breathe sweet melody,
    We may behold Her face who long ago
Dwelt among men by the Ægean sea,
    And whose sad house with pillaged portico   100
And friezeless wall and columns toppled down
Looms o'er the ruins of that fair and violet-cinctured town.

Spirit of Beauty! tarry still awhile,
    They are not dead, thine ancient votaries,
Some few there are to whom thy radiant smile
    Is better than a thousand victories,
Though all the nobly slain of Waterloo
Rise up in wrath against them! tarry still, there are a few

Who for thy sake would give their manlihood
    And consecrate their being, I at least   110
Have done so, made thy lips my daily food,
    And in thy temples found a goodlier feast
Than this starved age can give me, spite of all
Its new-found creeds so sceptical and so dogmatical.

Here not Cephissos, not Ilissos flows,
    The woods of white Colonos are not here,
On our bleak hills the olive never blows,
    No simple priest conducts his lowing steer
Up the steep marble way, nor through the town
Do laughing maidens bear to thee the crocus-flowered
        gown.   120

Yet tarry! for the boy who loved thee best,
    Whose very name should be a memory
To make thee linger, sleeps in silent rest
    Beneath the Roman walls, and melody
Still mourns her sweetest lyre, none can play
The lute of Adonis, with his lips Song passed away.

Nay, when Keats died the Muses still had left
    One silver voice to sing his threnody,
But ah! too soon of it we were bereft
    When on that riven night and stormy sea   130
Panthea claimed her singer as her own,
And slew the mouth that praised her; since which time we
        walk alone,

Save for that fiery heart, that morning star
    Of re-arisen England, whose clear eye
Saw from our tottering throne and waste of war
    The grand Greek limbs of young Democracy
Rise mightily like Hesperus and bring
The great Republic! him at least thy love hath taught to sing,

And he had been with thee at Thessaly,
    And seen white Atalanta fleet of foot   140
In passionless and fierce virginity
    Hunting the tuskèd boar, his honied lute
Hath pierced the cavern of the hollow hill,
And Venus laughs to know one knee will bow before her
    still.

And he hath kissed the lips of Proserpine,
    And sung the Galilæan's requiem,
That wounded forehead dashed with blood and wine
    He hath discrowned, the Ancient Gods in him
Have found their last, most ardent worshipper,
And the new Sign grows grey and dim before its conqueror.   150

Spirit of Beauty! tarry with us still,
    It is not quenched the torch of poesy,
The star that shook above the Eastern hill
    Holds unassailed its argent armoury
From all the gathering gloom and fretful fight –
O tarry with us still! for through the long and common
    night,

Morris, our sweet and simple Chaucer's child,
    Dear heritor of Spenser's tuneful reed,
With soft and sylvan pipe has oft beguiled
    The weary soul of man in troublous need,   160
And from the far and flowerless fields of ice
Has brought fair flowers to make an earthly paradise.

28

We know them all, Gudrun the strong men's bride,
    Aslaug and Olafson we know them all,
How giant Grettir fought and Sigurd died,
    And what enchantment held the king in thrall
When lonely Brynhild wrestled with the powers
That war against all passion, ah! how oft through summer
        hours,

Long listless summer hours when the noon
    Being enamoured of a damask rose   170
Forgets to journey westward, till the moon
    The pale usurper of its tribute grows
From a thin sickle to a silver shield
And chides its loitering car – how oft, in some cool grassy
        field

Far from the cricket-ground and noisy eight,
    At Bagley, where the rustling bluebells come
Almost before the blackbird finds a mate
    And overstay the swallow, and the hum
Of many murmuring bees flits through the leaves,
Have I lain poring on the dreamy tales his fancy weaves,   180

And through their unreal woes and mimic pain
    Wept for myself, and so was purified,
And in their simple mirth grew glad again;
    For as I sailed upon that pictured tide
The strength and splendour of the storm was mine
Without the storm's red ruin, for the singer is divine,

The little laugh of water falling down
    Is not so musical, the clammy gold
Close hoarded in the tiny waxen town
    Has less of sweetness in it, and the old   190
Half-withered reeds that waved in Arcady
Touched by his lips break forth again to fresher harmony.

Spirit of Beauty, tarry yet awhile!
    Although the cheating merchants of the mart
With iron roads profane our lovely isle,
    And break on whirling wheels the limbs of Art,
Ay! though the crowded factories beget
The blindworm Ignorance that slays the soul, O tarry yet!

For One at least there is, – He bears his name
    From Dante and the seraph Gabriel, –   200
Whose double laurels burn with deathless flame
    To light thine altar; He too loves thee well,
Who saw old Merlin lured in Vivien's snare,
And the white feet of angels coming down the golden stair,

Loves thee so well, that all the World for him
    A gorgeous-coloured vestiture must wear,
And Sorrow take a purple diadem,
    Or else be no more Sorrow, and Despair
Gild its own thorns, and Pain, like Adon, be
Even in anguish beautiful; – such is the empery   210

Which Painters hold, and such the heritage
    This gentle solemn Spirit doth possess,
Being a better mirror of his age
    In all his pity, love, and weariness,
Than those who can but copy common things,
And leave the Soul unpainted with its mighty questionings.

But they are few, and all romance has flown,
    And men can prophesy about the sun,
And lecture on his arrows – how, alone,
    Through a waste void the soulless atoms run,   220
How from each tree its weeping nymph has fled,
And that no more 'mid English reeds a Naïad shows her
        head.

Methinks these new Actæons boast too soon
    That they have spied on beauty; what if we
Have analysed the rainbow, robbed the moon
    Of her most ancient, chastest mystery,
Shall I, the last Endymion, lose all hope
Because rude eyes peer at my mistress through a telescope!

What profit if this scientific age
    Burst through our gates with all its retinue   230
Of modern miracles! Can it assuage
    One lover's breaking heart? what can it do
To make one life more beautiful, one day
More godlike in its period? but now the Age of Clay

Returns in horrid cycle, and the earth
    Hath borne again a noisy progeny
Of ignorant Titans, whose ungodly birth
    Hurls them against the august hierarchy
Which sat upon Olympus, to the Dust
They have appealed, and to that barren arbiter they must   240

Repair for judgment, let them, if they can,
    From Natural Warfare and insensate Chance,
Create the new Ideal rule for man!
    Methinks that was not my inheritance;
For I was nurtured otherwise, my soul
Passes from higher heights of life to a more supreme goal.

Lo! while we spake the earth did turn away
    Her visage from the God, and Hecate's boat
Rose silver-laden, till the jealous day
    Blew all its torches out: I did not note   250
The waning hours, to young Endymions
Time's palsied fingers count in vain his rosary of suns!

Mark how the yellow iris wearily
    Leans back its throat, as though it would be kissed
By its false chamberer, the dragon-fly,
    Who, like a blue vein on a girl's white wrist,
Sleeps on that snowy primrose of the night,
Which 'gins to flush with crimson shame, and die beneath
        the light.

Come let us go, against the pallid shield
    Of the wan sky the almond blossoms gleam,   260
The corncrake nested in the unmown field
    Answers its mate, across the misty stream
On fitful wing the startled curlews fly,
And in his sedgy bed the lark, for joy that Day is nigh,

Scatters the pearlèd dew from off the grass,
    In tremulous ecstasy to greet the sun,
Who soon in gilded panoply will pass
    Forth from yon orange-curtained pavilion
Hung in the burning east, see, the red rim
O'ertops the expectant hills! it is the God! for love of him   270

Already the shrill lark is out of sight,
    Flooding with waves of song this silent dell, –
Ah! there is something more in that bird's flight
    Than could be tested in a crucible! –
But the air freshens, let us go, why soon
The woodmen will be here; how we have lived this night
        of June!

Requiescat

Tread lightly, she is near
   Under the snow,
Speak gently, she can hear
   The daisies grow.

All her bright golden hair
   Tarnished with rust,
She that was young and fair
   Fallen to dust.

Lily-like, white as snow,
   She hardly knew
She was a woman, so
   Sweetly she grew.

Coffin-board, heavy stone,
   Lie on her breast,
I vex my heart alone,
   She is at rest.

Peace, Peace, she cannot hear
   Lyre or sonnet,
All my life's buried here,
   Heap earth upon it.

Avignon

Sonnet

on hearing the Dies Iræ sung in the Sistine Chapel

Nay, Lord, not thus! white lilies in the spring,
   Sad olive-groves, or silver-breasted dove,
   Teach me more clearly of Thy life and love
Than terrors of red flame and thundering.
The hillside vines dear memories of Thee bring:
   A bird at evening flying to its nest
   Tells me of One who had no place of rest:
I think it is of Thee the sparrows sing.
Come rather on some autumn afternoon,
   When red and brown are burnished on the leaves,
   And the fields echo to the gleaner's song,
Come when the splendid fulness of the moon,
   Looks down upon the rows of golden sheaves,
   And reap Thy harvest: we have waited long.

The Burden of Itys

This English Thames is holier far than Rome,
   Those harebells like a sudden flash of sea
Breaking across the woodland, with the foam
   Of meadow-sweet and white anemone
To fleck their blue waves, – God is likelier there
Than hidden in that crystal-hearted star the pale monks
    bear!

Those violet-gleaming butterflies that take
   Yon creamy lily for their pavilion
Are monsignores, and where the rushes shake
   A lazy pike lies basking in the sun,   10
His eyes half shut, – He is some mitred old
Bishop *in partibus*! look at those gaudy scales all green and
    gold.

The wind the restless prisoner of the trees
   Does well for Palæstrina, one would say
The mighty master's hands were on the keys
   Of the Maria organ, which they play
When early on some sapphire Easter morn
In a high litter red as blood or sin the Pope is borne

From his dark House out to the Balcony
   Above the bronze gates and the crowded square,   20
Whose very fountains seem for ecstasy
   To toss their silver lances in the air,
And stretching out weak hands to East and West
In vain sends peace to peaceless lands, to restless nations
    rest.

Is not yon lingering orange after-glow
   That stays to vex the moon more fair than all
Rome's lordliest pageants! strange, a year ago
   I knelt before some crimson Cardinal
Who bare the Host across the Esquiline,
And now – those common poppies in the wheat seem twice
    as fine.   30

The blue-green beanfields yonder, tremulous
   With the last shower, sweeter perfume bring
Through this cool evening than the odorous
   Flame-jewelled censers the young deacons swing,
When the grey priest unlocks the curtained shrine,
And makes God's body from the common fruit of corn and
    vine.

Poor Fra Giovanni bawling at the mass
   Were out of tune now, for a small brown bird
Sings overhead, and through the long cool grass
   I see that throbbing throat which once I heard   40
On starlit hills of flower-starred Arcady,
Once where the white and crescent sand of Salamis meets
    sea.

Sweet is the swallow twittering on the eaves
    At daybreak, when the mower whets his scythe,
And stock-doves murmur, and the milkmaid leaves
    Her little lonely bed, and carols blithe
To see the heavy-lowing cattle wait
Stretching their huge and dripping mouths across the
        farmyard gate.

And sweet the hops upon the Kentish leas,
    And sweet the wind that lifts the new-mown hay,   50
And sweet the fretful swarms of grumbling bees
    That round and round the linden blossoms play;
And sweet the heifer breathing in the stall,
And the green bursting figs that hang upon the red-brick
        wall.

And sweet to hear the cuckoo mock the spring
    While the last violet loiters by the well,
And sweet to hear the shepherd Daphnis sing
    The song of Linus through a sunny dell
Of warm Arcadia where the corn is gold
And the slight lithe-limbed reapers dance about the wattled
        fold.   60

And sweet with young Lycoris to recline
    In some Illyrian valley far away,
Where canopied on herbs amaracine
    We too might waste the summer-trancèd day
Matching our reeds in sportive rivalry,
While far beneath us frets the troubled purple of the sea.

But sweeter far if silver-sandalled foot
    Of some long-hidden God should ever tread
The Nuneham meadows, if with reeded flute
    Pressed to his lips some Faun might raise his head   70
By the green water-flags, ah! sweet indeed
To see the heavenly herdsman call his white-fleeced flock
        to feed.

Then sing to me thou tuneful chorister,
    Though what thou sing'st be thine own requiem!
Tell me thy tale thou hapless chronicler
    Of thine own tragedies! do not contemn
These unfamiliar haunts, this English field,
For many a lovely coronal our northern isle can yield

Which Grecian meadows know not, many a rose
    Which all day long in vales Æolian   80
A lad might seek in vain for over-grows
    Our hedges like a wanton courtesan
Unthrifty of its beauty, lilies too
Ilissus never mirrored star our streams, and cockles blue

Dot the green wheat which, though they are the signs
    For swallows going south, would never spread
Their azure tents between the Attic vines;
    Even that little weed of ragged red,
Which bids the robin pipe, in Arcady
Would be a trespasser, and many an unsung elegy   90

Sleeps in the reeds that fringe our winding Thames
    Which to awake were sweeter ravishment
Than ever Syrinx wept for, diadems
    Of brown bee-studded orchids which were meant
For Cytheræa's brows are hidden here
Unknown to Cytheræa, and by yonder pasturing steer

There is a tiny yellow daffodil,
    The butterfly can see it from afar,
Although one summer evening's dew could fill
    Its little cup twice over ere the star   100
Had called the lazy shepherd to his fold
And be no prodigal, each leaf is flecked with spotted gold

As if Jove's gorgeous leman Danae
   Hot from his gilded arms had stooped to kiss
The trembling petals, or young Mercury
   Low-flying to the dusky ford of Dis
Had with one feather of his pinions
Just brushed them! the slight stem which bears the burden
    of its suns

Is hardly thicker than the gossamer,
   Or poor Arachne's silver tapestry, –   110
Men say it bloomed upon the sepulchre
   Of One I sometime worshipped, but to me
It seems to bring diviner memories
Of faun-loved Heliconian glades and blue nymph-haunted
    seas,

Of an untrodden vale at Tempe where
   On the clear river's marge Narcissus lies,
The tangle of the forest in his hair,
   The silence of the woodland in his eyes,
Wooing that drifting imagery which is
No sooner kissed than broken, memories of Salmacis   120

Who is not boy or girl and yet is both,
   Fed by two fires and unsatisfied
Through their excess, each passion being loth
   For love's own sake to leave the other's side
Yet killing love by staying, memories
Of Oreads peeping through the leaves of silent moonlit
    trees,

Of lonely Ariadne on the wharf
   At Naxos, when she saw the treacherous crew
Far out at sea, and waved her crimson scarf
   And called false Theseus back again nor knew   130
That Dionysos on an amber pard
Was close behind her, memories of what Mæonia's bard

With sightless eyes beheld, the wall of Troy,
    Queen Helen lying in the ivory room,
And at her side an amorous red-lipped boy
    Trimming with dainty hand his helmet's plume,
And far away the moil, the shout, the groan,
As Hector shielded off the spear and Ajax hurled the stone;

Of wingèd Perseus with his flawless sword
    Cleaving the snaky tresses of the witch,   140
And all those tales imperishably stored
    In little Grecian urns, freightage more rich
Than any gaudy galleon of Spain
Bare from the Indies ever! these at least bring back again,

For well I know they are not dead at all,
    The ancient Gods of Grecian poesy,
They are asleep, and when they hear thee call
    Will wake and think 't is very Thessaly,
This Thames the Daulian waters, this cool glade
The yellow-irised mead where once young Itys laughed
        and played.   150

If it was thou dear jasmine-cradled bird
    Who from the leafy stillness of thy throne
Sang to the wondrous boy, until he heard
    The horn of Atalanta faintly blown
Across the Cumnor hills, and wandering
Through Bagley wood at evening found the Attic poets'
        spring, –

Ah! tiny sober-suited advocate
    That pleadest for the moon against the day!
If thou didst make the shepherd seek his mate
    On that sweet questing, when Proserpina   160
Forgot it was not Sicily and leant
Across the mossy Sandford stile in ravished wonderment, –

Light-winged and bright-eyed miracle of the wood!
    If ever thou didst soothe with melody
One of that little clan, that brotherhood
    Which loved the morning-star of Tuscany
More than the perfect sun of Raphael
And is immortal, sing to me! for I too love thee well,

Sing on! sing on! let the dull world grow young,
    Let elemental things take form again,   170
And the old shapes of Beauty walk among
    The simple garths and open crofts, as when
The son of Leto bare the willow rod,
And the soft sheep and shaggy goats followed the boyish
        God.

Sing on! sing on! the Bacchus will be here
    Astride upon his gorgeous Indian throne,
And over whimpering tigers shake the spear
    With yellow ivy crowned and gummy cone,
While at his side the wanton Bassarid
Will throw the lion by the mane and catch the mountain kid!   180

Sing on! and I will wear the leopard skin,
    And steam the moonèd wings of Ashtaroth,
Upon whose icy chariot we could win
    Cithæron in an hour ere the froth
Has over-brimmed the wine-vat or the Faun
Ceased from the treading! ay, before the flickering lamp
        of dawn

Has scared the hooting owlet to its nest,
    And warned the bat to close its filmy vans,
Some Mænad girl with vine-leaves on her breast
    Will filch their beech-nuts from the sleeping Pans   190
So softly that the little nested thrush
Will never wake, and then with shrilly laugh and leap will
        rush

Down the green valley where the fallen dew
    Lies thick beneath the elm and count her store,
Till the brown Satyrs in a jolly crew
    Trample the loosestrife down along the shore,
And where their hornèd master sits in state
Bring strawberries and bloomy plums upon a wicker crate!

Sing on! and soon with passion-wearied face
    Through the cool leaves Apollo's lad will come,   200
The Tyrian prince his bristled boar will chase
    Adown the chestnut-copses all a-bloom,
And ivory-limbed, grey-eyed, with look of pride,
After yon velvet-coated deer the virgin maid will ride.

Sing on! and I the dying boy will see
    Stain with his purple blood the waxen bell
That overweighs the jacinth, and to me
    The wretched Cyprian her woe will tell,
And I will kiss her mouth and streaming eyes,
And lead her to the myrtle-hidden grove where Adon lies!   210

Cry out aloud on Itys! memory
    That foster-brother of remorse and pain
Drops poison in mine ear, – O to be free,
    To burn one's old ships! and to launch again
Into the white-plumed battle of the waves
And fight old Proteus for the spoil of coral-flowered caves!

O for Medea with her poppied spell!
    O for the secret of the Colchian shrine!
O for one leaf of that pale asphodel
    Which binds the tired brows of Proserpine,   220
And sheds such wondrous dews at eve that she
Dreams of the fields of Enna, by the far Sicilian sea,

Where oft the golden-girdled bee she chased
    From lily to lily on the level mead,
Ere yet her sombre Lord had bid her taste
    The deadly fruit of that pomegranate seed,
Ere the black steeds had harried her away
Down to the faint and flowerless land, the sick and sunless
      day.

O for one midnight and as paramour
    The Venus of the little Melian farm!   230
O that some antique statue for one hour
    Might wake to passion, and that I could charm
The Dawn at Florence from its dumb despair,
Mix with those mighty limbs and make that giant breast
      my lair!

Sing on! sing on! I would be drunk with life,
    Drunk with the trampled vintage of my youth,
I would forget the wearying wasted strife,
    The riven veil, the Gorgon eyes of Truth,
The prayerless vigil and the cry for prayer,
The barren gifts, the lifted arms, the dull insensate air!   240

Sing on! sing on! O feathered Niobe,
    Thou canst make sorrow beautiful, and steal
From joy its sweetest music, not as we
    Who by dead voiceless silence strive to heal
Our too untented wounds, and do but keep
Pain barricadoed in our hearts, and murder pillowed sleep.

Sing louder yet, why must I still behold
    The wan white face of that deserted Christ,
Whose bleeding hands my hands did once enfold,
    Whose smitten lips my lips so oft have kissed,   250
And now in mute and marble misery
Sits in his lone dishonoured House and weeps, perchance
      for me?

O Memory cast down thy wreathèd shell!
   Break thy hoarse lute O sad Melpomene!
O Sorrow, Sorrow keep thy cloistered cell
   Nor dim with tears this limpid Castaly!
Cease, Philomel, thou dost the forest wrong
To vex its sylvan quiet with such wild impassioned song!

Cease, cease, or if 't is anguish to be dumb
   Take from the pastoral thrush her simpler air,   260
Whose jocund carelessness doth more become
   This English woodland than thy keen despair,
Ah! cease and let the north wind bear thy lay
Back to the rocky hills of Thrace, the stormy Daulian bay.

A moment more, the startled leaves had stirred,
   Endymion would have passed across the mead
Moonstruck with love, and this still Thames had heard
   Pan plash and paddle groping for some reed
To lure from her blue cave that Naiad maid
Who for such piping listens half in joy and half afraid.   270

A moment more, the waking dove had cooed,
   The silver daughter of the silver sea
With the fond gyves of clinging hands had wooed
   Her wanton from the chase, and Dryope
Had thrust aside the branches of her oak
To see the lusty gold-haired lad rein in his snorting yoke.

A moment more, the trees had stooped to kiss
   Pale Daphne just awakening from the swoon
Of tremulous laurels, lonely Salmacis
   Had bared his barren beauty to the moon,   280
And through the vale with sad voluptuous smile
Antinous had wandered, the red lotus of the Nile

Down leaning from his black and clustering hair,
　　To shade those slumberous eyelids' caverned bliss,
Or else on yonder grassy slope with bare
　　High-tuniced limbs unravished Artemis
Had bade her hounds give tongue, and roused the deer
From his green ambuscade with shrill halloo and pricking
　　　　spear.

Lie still, lie still, O passionate heart, lie still!
　　O Melancholy, fold thy raven wing!　　　　　　　　　　　290
O sobbing Dryad, from thy hollow hill
　　Come not with such despondent answering!
No more thou wingèd Marsyas complain,
Apollo loveth not to hear such troubled songs of pain!

It was a dream, the glade is tenantless,
　　No soft Ionian laughter moves the air,
The Thames creeps on in sluggish leadenness,
　　And from the copse left desolate and bare
Fled is young Bacchus with his revelry,
Yet still from Nuneham wood there comes that thrilling
　　　　melody　　　　　　　　　　　　　　　　　　　　300

So sad, that one might think a human heart
　　Brake in each separate note, a quality
Which music sometimes has, being the Art
　　Which is most nigh to tears and memory,
Poor mourning Philomel, what dost thou fear?
Thy sister doth not haunt these fields, Pandion is not here,

Here is no cruel Lord with murderous blade,
　　No woven web of bloody heraldries,
But mossy dells for roving comrades made,
　　Warm valleys where the tired student lies　　　　　　　310
With half-shut book, and many a winding walk
Where rustic lovers stray at eve in happy simple talk.

The harmless rabbit gambols with its young
    Across the trampled towing-path, where late
A troop of laughing boys in jostling throng
    Cheered with their noisy cries the racing eight;
The gossamer, with ravelled silver threads,
Works at its little loom, and from the dusky red-eaved
        sheds

Of the lone Farm a flickering light shines out
    Where the swinked shepherd drives his bleating flock   320
Back to their wattled sheep-cotes, a faint shout
    Comes from some Oxford boat at Sandford lock,
And starts the moor-hen from the sedgy rill,
And the dim lengthening shadows flit like swallows up
        the hill.

The heron passes homeward to the mere,
    The blue mist creeps among the shivering trees,
Gold world by world the silent stars appear,
    And like a blossom blown before the breeze
A white moon drifts across the shimmering sky,
Mute arbitress of all thy sad, thy rapturous threnody.   330

She does not heed thee, wherefore should she heed,
    She knows Endymion is not far away,
'Tis I, 'tis I, whose soul is as the reed
    Which has no message of its own to play,
So pipes another's bidding, it is I,
Drifting with every wind on the wide sea of misery.

Ah! the brown bird has ceased: one exquisite trill
    About the sombre woodland seems to cling
Dying in music, else the air is still,
    So still that one might hear the bat's small wing   340
Wander and wheel above the pines, or tell
Each tiny dew-drop dripping from the bluebell's brimming
        cell.

45

And far away across the lengthening wold,
   Across the willowy flats and thickets brown,
Magdalen's tall tower tipped with tremulous gold
   Marks the long High Street of the little town,
And warns me to return; I must not wait,
Hark! 'tis the curfew booming from the bell at Christ Church gate.

Impression du Matin

The Thames nocturne of blue and gold
   Changed to a Harmony in grey:
   A barge with ochre-coloured hay
Dropt from the wharf: and chill and cold

The yellow fog came creeping down
   The bridges, till the houses' walls
   Seemed changed to shadows and St Paul's
Loomed like a bubble o'er the town.

Then suddenly arose the clang
   Of waking life; the streets were stirred
   With country waggons: and a bird
Flew to the glistening roofs and sang.

But one pale woman all alone,
   The daylight kissing her wan hair,
   Loitered beneath the gas lamps' flare,
With lips of flame and heart of stone.

Charmides

I

He was a Grecian lad, who coming home
   With pulpy figs and wine from Sicily
Stood at his galley's prow, and let the foam
   Blow through his crisp brown curls unconsciously,
And holding wave and wind in boy's despite
Peered from his dripping seat across the wet and stormy
      night

Till with the dawn he saw a burnished spear
   Like a thin thread of gold against the sky,
And hoisted sail, and strained the creaking gear,
   And bade the pilot head her lustily   10
Against the nor'west gale, and all day long
Held on his way, and marked the rowers' time with
      measured song,

And when the faint Corinthian hills were red
   Dropped anchor in a little sandy bay,
And with fresh boughs of olive crowned his head,
   And brushed from cheek and throat the hoary spray,
And washed his limbs with oil, and from the hold
Brought out his linen tunic and his sandals brazen-soled,

And a rich robe stained with the fishes' juice
   Which of some swarthy trader he had bought   20
Upon the sunny quay at Syracuse,
   And was with Tyrian broideries inwrought,
And by the questioning merchants made his way
Up through the soft and silver woods, and when the
      labouring day

Had spun its tangled web of crimson cloud,
    Clomb the high hill, and with swift silent feet
Crept to the fane unnoticed by the crowd
    Of busy priests, and from some dark retreat
Watched the young swains his frolic playmates bring
The firstling of their little flock, and the shy shepherd fling   30

The crackling salt upon the flame, or hang
    His studded crook against the temple wall
To Her who keeps away the ravenous fang
    Of the base wolf from homestead and from stall;
And then the clear-voiced maidens 'gan to sing,
And to the altar each man brought some goodly offering,

A beechen cup brimming with milky foam,
    A fair cloth wrought with cunning imagery
Of hounds in chase, a waxen honey-comb
    Dripping with oozy gold which scarce the bee   40
Had ceased from building, a black skin of oil
Meet for the wrestlers, a great boar the fierce and
        white-tusked spoil

Stolen from Artemis that jealous maid
    To please Athena, and the dappled hide
Of a tall stag who in some mountain glade
    Had met the shaft; and then the herald cried,
And from the pillared precinct one by one
Went the glad Greeks well pleased that they their simple
        vows had done.

And the old priest put out the waning fires
    Save that one lamp whose restless ruby glowed   50
For ever in the cell, and the shrill lyres
    Came fainter on the wind, as down the road
In joyous dance these country folk did pass,
And with stout hands the warder closed the gates of
        polished brass.

48

Long time he lay and hardly dared to breathe,
    And heard the cadenced drip of spilt-out wine,
And the rose-petals falling from the wreath
    As the night breezes wandered through the shrine,
And seemed to be in some entrancèd swoon
Till through the open roof above the full and brimming
        moon   60

Flooded with sheeny waves the marble floor,
    When from his nook up leapt the venturous lad,
And flinging wide the cedar-carven door
    Beheld an awful image saffron-clad
And armed for battle! the gaunt Griffin glared
From the huge helm, and the long lance of wreck and ruin
        flared

Like a red rod of flame, stony and steeled
    The Gorgon's head its leaden eyeballs rolled,
And writhed its snaky horrors through the shield,
    And gaped aghast with bloodless lips and cold   70
In passion impotent, while with blind gaze
The blinking owl between the feet hooted in shrill amaze.

The lonely fisher as he trimmed his lamp
    Far out at sea off Sunium, or cast
The net for tunnies, heard a brazen tramp
    Of horses smite the waves, and a wild blast
Divide the folded curtains of the night,
And knelt upon the little poop, and prayed in holy fright.

And guilty lovers in their venery
    Forgat a little while their stolen sweets,   80
Deeming they heard dread Dian's bitter cry;
    And the grim watchmen on their lofty seats
Ran to their shields in haste precipitate,
Or strained black-bearded throats across the dusky parapet.

For round the temple rolled the clang of arms,
  And the twelve Gods leapt up in marble fear,
And the air quaked with dissonant alarums
  Till huge Poseidon shook his mighty spear,
And on the frieze the prancing horses neighed,
And the low tread of hurrying feet rang from the cavalcade.   90

Ready for death with parted lips he stood,
  And well content at such a price to see
That calm wide brow, that terrible maidenhood,
  The marvel of that pitiless chastity,
Ah! well content indeed, for never wight
Since Troy's young shepherd prince had seen so wonderful
    a sight.

Ready for death he stood, but lo! the air
  Grew silent, and the horses ceased to neigh,
And off his brow he tossed the clustering hair,
  And from his limbs he threw the cloak away,   100
For whom would not such love make desperate,
And nigher came, and touched her throat, and with hands
    violate

Undid the cuirass, and the crocus gown,
  And bared the breasts of polished ivory,
Till from the waist the peplos falling down
  Left visible the secret mystery
Which to no lover will Athena show,
The grand cool flanks, the crescent thighs, the bossy hills
    of snow.

Those who have never known a lover's sin
  Let them not read my ditty, it will be   110
To their dull ears so musicless and thin
  That they will have no joy of it, but ye
To whose wan cheeks now creeps the lingering smile,
Ye who have learned who Eros is, – O listen yet awhile.

A little space he let his greedy eyes
　　Rest on the burnished image, till mere sight
Half swooned for surfeit of such luxuries,
　　And then his lips in hungering delight
Fed on her lips, and round the towered neck
He flung his arms, nor cared at all his passion's will to check.　　120

Never I ween did lover hold such tryst,
　　For all night long he murmured honeyed word,
And saw her sweet unravished limbs, and kissed
　　Her pale and argent body undisturbed,
And paddled with the polished throat, and pressed
His hot and beating heart upon her chill and icy breast.

It was as if Numidian javelins
　　Pierced through and through his wild and whirling brain,
And his nerves thrilled like throbbing violins
　　In exquisite pulsation, and the pain　　　　　　　　130
Was such sweet anguish that he never drew
His lips from hers till overhead the lark of warning flew.

They who have never seen the daylight peer
　　Into a darkened room, and drawn the curtain,
And with dull eyes and wearied from some dear
　　And worshipped body risen, they for certain
Will never know of what I try to sing,
How long the last kiss was, how fond and late his lingering.

The moon was girdled with a crystal rim,
　　The sign which shipmen say is ominous　　　　　　140
Of wrath in heaven, the wan stars were dim,
　　And the low lightening east was tremulous
With the faint fluttering wings of flying dawn,
Ere from the silent sombre shrine this lover had withdrawn.

Down the steep rock with hurried feet and fast
   Clomb the brave lad, and reached the cave of Pan,
And heard the goat-foot snoring as he passed,
   And leapt upon a grassy knoll and ran
Like a young fawn unto an olive wood
Which in a shady valley by the well-built city stood.   150

And sought a little stream, which well he knew,
   For oftentimes with boyish careless shout
The green and crested grebe he would pursue,
   Or snare in woven net the silver trout,
And down amid the startled reeds he lay
Panting in breathless sweet affright, and waited for the day.

On the green bank he lay, and let one hand
   Dip in the cool dark eddies listlessly,
And soon the breath of morning came and fanned
   His hot flushed cheeks, or lifted wantonly   160
The tangled curls from off his forehead, while
He on the running water gazed with strange and secret
     smile.

And soon the shepherd in rough woollen cloak
   With his long crook undid the wattled cotes,
And from the stack a thin blue wreath of smoke
   Curled through the air across the ripening oats,
And on the hill the yellow house-dog bayed
As through the crisp and rustling fern the heavy cattle
     strayed.

And when the light-foot mower went afield
   Across the meadows laced with threaded dew,   170
And the sheep bleated on the misty weald,
   And from its nest the waking corncrake flew,
Some woodmen saw him lying by the stream
And marvelled much that any lad so beautiful could seem,

Nor deemed him born of mortals, and one said,
   'It is young Hylas, that false runaway
Who with a Naiad now would make his bed
   Forgetting Herakles,' but others, 'Nay,
It is Narcissus, his own paramour,
Those are the fond and crimson lips no woman can allure.'   180

And when they nearer came a third one cried,
   'It is young Dionysos who has hid
His spear and fawnskin by the river side
   Weary of hunting with the Bassarid,
And wise indeed were we away to fly
They live not long who on the gods immortal come to spy.'

So turned they back, and feared to look behind,
   And told the timid swain how they had seen
Amid the reeds some woodland God reclined,
   And no man dared to cross the open green,   190
And on that day no olive-tree was slain,
Nor rushes cut, but all deserted was the fair domain,

Save when the neat-herd's lad, his empty pail
   Well slung upon his back, with leap and bound
Raced on the other side, and stopped to hail,
   Hoping that he some comrade new had found,
And gat no answer, and then half afraid
Passed on his simple way, or down the still and silent glade

A little girl ran laughing from the farm,
   Not thinking of love's secret mysteries,   200
And when she saw the white and gleaming arm
   And all his manlihood, with longing eyes
Whose passion mocked her sweet virginity
Watched him awhile, and then stole back sadly and wearily.

Far off he heard the city's hum and noise,
    And now and then the shriller laughter where
The passionate purity of brown-limbed boys
    Wrestled or raced in the clear healthful air,
And now and then a little tinkling bell
As the shorn wether led the sheep down to the mossy well.   210

Through the grey willows danced the fretful gnat,
    The grasshopper chirped idly from the tree,
In sleek and oily coat the water-rat
    Breasting the little ripples manfully
Made for the wild-duck's nest, from bough to bough
Hopped the shy finch, and the huge tortoise crept across
        the slough.

On the faint wind floated the silky seeds
    As the bright scythe swept through the waving grass,
The ousel-cock splashed circles in the reeds
    And flecked with silver whorls the forest's glass,   220
Which scarce had caught again its imagery
Ere from its bed the dusky tench leapt at the dragon-fly.

But little care had he for any thing
    Though up and down the beech the squirrel played,
And from the copse the linnet 'gan to sing
    To her brown mate her sweetest serenade;
Ah! little care indeed, for he had seen
The breasts of Pallas and the naked wonder of the Queen.

But when the herdsman called his straggling goats
    With whistling pipe across the rocky road,   230
And the shard-beetle with its trumpet-notes
    Boomed through the darkening woods, and seemed to bode
Of coming storm, and the belated crane
Passed homeward like a shadow, and the dull big drops of
        rain

Fell on the pattering fig-leaves, up he rose
   And from the gloomy forest went his way
Past sombre homestead and wet orchard-close,
   And came at last unto a little quay,
And called his mates aboard, and took his seat
On the high poop, and pushed from land, and loosed the
     dripping sheet,   240

And steered across the bay, and when nine suns
   Passed down the long and laddered way of gold,
And nine pale moons had breathed their orisons
   To the chaste stars their confessors, or told
Their dearest secret to the downy moth
That will not fly at noonday, through the foam and surging
     froth

Came a great owl with yellow sulphurous eyes
   And lit upon the ship, whose timbers creaked
As though the lading of three argosies
   Were in the hold, and flapped its wings and shrieked,   250
And darkness straightway stole across the deep,
Sheathed was Orion's sword, dread Mars himself fled down
     the steep,

And the moon hid behind a tawny mask
   Of drifting cloud, and from the ocean's marge
Rose the red plume, the huge and hornèd casque,
   The seven-cubit spear, the brazen targe!
And clad in bright and burnished panoply
Athena strode across the stretch of sick and shivering sea!

To the dull sailors' sight her loosened locks
   Seemed like the jagged storm-rack, and her feet   260
Only the spume that floats on hidden rocks,
   And, marking how the rising waters beat
Against the rolling ship, the pilot cried
To the young helmsman at the stern to luff to windward side.

55

But he, the overbold adulterer,
    A dear profaner of great mysteries,
An ardent amorous idolater,
    When he beheld those grand relentless eyes
Laughed loud for joy, and crying out 'I come'
Leapt from the lofty poop into the chill and churning foam.   270

Then fell from the high heaven one bright star,
    One dancer left the circling galaxy,
And back to Athens on her clattering car
    In all the pride of venged divinity
Pale Pallas swept with shrill and stately clank,
And a few gurgling bubbles rose where her boy lover sank.

And the mast shuddered as the gaunt owl flew
    With mocking hoots after the wrathful Queen,
And the old pilot bade the trembling crew
    Hoist the big sail, and told how he had seen   280
Close to the stern a dim and giant form,
And like a dipping swallow the stout ship dashed through
        the storm.

And no man dared to speak of Charmides
    Deeming that he some evil thing had wrought,
And when they reached the strait Symplegades
    They beached their galley on the shore, and sought
The toll-gate of the city hastily,
And in the market showed their brown and pictured pottery.

II

But some good Triton-god had ruth, and bare
    The boy's drowned body back to Grecian land,   290
And mermaids combed his dank and dripping hair
    And smoothed his brow, and loosed his clenching hand,
Some brought sweet spices from far Araby,
And others bade the halcyon sing her softest lullaby.

And when he neared his old Athenian home,
   A mighty billow rose up suddenly
Upon whose oily back the clotted foam
   Lay diapered in some strange fantasy,
And clasping him unto its glassy breast
Swept landward, like a white-maned steed upon a
      venturous quest!   300

Now where Colonos leans unto the sea
   There lies a long and level stretch of lawn,
The rabbit knows it, and the mountain bee
   For it deserts Hymettus, and the Faun
Is not afraid, for never through the day
Comes a cry ruder than the shout of shepherd lads at play.

But often from the thorny labyrinth
   And tangled branches of the circling wood
The stealthy hunter sees young Hyacinth
   Hurling the polished disk, and draws his hood   310
Over his guilty gaze, and creeps away,
Nor dares to wind his horn, or – else at the first break of day

The Dryads come and throw the leathern ball
   Along the reedy shore, and circumvent
Some goat-eared Pan to be their seneschal
   For fear of bold Poseidon's ravishment,
And loose their girdles, with shy timorous eyes,
Lest from the surf his azure arms and purple beard should
      rise.

On this side and on that a rocky cave,
   Hung with the yellow-belled laburnum, stands,   320
Smooth is the beach, save where some ebbing wave
   Leaves its faint outline etched upon the sands,
As though it feared to be too soon forgot
By the green rush, its playfellow, – and yet, it is a spot

So small, that the inconstant butterfly
    Could steal the hoarded honey from each flower
Ere it was noon, and still not satisfy
    Its over-greedy love, – within an hour
A sailor boy, were he but rude enow
To land and pluck a garland for his galley's painted prow,   330

Would almost leave the little meadow bare,
    For it knows nothing of great pageantry,
Only a few narcissi here and there
    Stand separate in sweet austerity,
Dotting the un-mown grass with silver stars,
And here and there a daffodil waves tiny scimitars.

Hither the billow brought him, and was glad
    Of such dear servitude, and where the land
Was virgin of all waters laid the lad
    Upon the golden margent of the strand,   340
And like a lingering lover oft returned
To kiss those pallid limbs which once with intense fire
        burned,

Ere the wet seas had quenched that holocaust,
    That self-fed flame, that passionate lustihead,
Ere grisly death with chill and nipping frost
    Had withered up those lilies white and red
Which, while the boy would through the forest range,
Answered each other in a sweet antiphonal counter-change.

And when at dawn the wood-nymphs, hand-in-hand,
    Threaded the bosky dell, their satyr spied   350
The boy's pale body stretched upon the sand,
    And feared Poseidon's treachery, and cried,
And like bright sunbeams flitting through a glade
Each startled Dryad sought some safe and leafy ambuscade,

Save one white girl, who deemed it would not be
  So dread a thing to feel a sea-god's arms
Crushing her breasts in amorous tyranny,
  And longed to listen to those subtle charms
Insidious lovers weave when they would win
Some fencèd fortress, and stole back again, nor thought
      it sin   360

To yield her treasure unto one so fair,
  And lay beside him, thirsty with love's drouth,
Called him soft names, played with his tangled hair,
  And with hot lips made havoc of his mouth
Afraid he might not wake, and then afraid
Lest he might wake too soon, fled back, and then, fond
      renegade,

Returned to fresh assault, and all day long
  Sat at his side, and laughed at her new toy,
And held his hand, and sang her sweetest song,
  Then frowned to see how froward was the boy   370
Who would not with her maidenhood entwine,
Nor knew that three days since his eyes had looked on
      Proserpine,

Nor knew what sacrilege his lips had done,
  But said, 'He will awake, I know him well,
He will awake at evening when the sun
  Hangs his red shield on Corinth's citadel,
This sleep is but a cruel treachery
To make me love him more, and in some cavern of the sea

Deeper than ever falls the fisher's line
  Already a huge Triton blows his horn,   380
And weaves a garland from the crystalline
  And drifting ocean-tendrils to adorn
The emerald pillars of our bridal bed,
For sphered in foaming silver, and with coral-crownèd head,

We two will sit upon a throne of pearl,
  And a blue wave will be our canopy,
And at our feet the water-snakes will curl
  In all their amethystine panoply
Of diamonded mail, and we will mark
The mullets swimming by the mast of some storm-
    foundered bark,   390

Vermilion-finned with eyes of bossy gold
  Like flakes of crimson light, and the great deep
His glassy-portaled chamber will unfold,
  And we will see the painted dolphins sleep
Cradled by murmuring halcyons on the rocks
Where Proteus in quaint suit of green pastures his monstrous
    flocks.

And tremulous opal-hued anemones
  Will wave their purple fringes where we tread
Upon the mirrored floor, and argosies
  Of fishes flecked with tawny scales will thread   400
The drifting cordage of the shattered wreck,
And honey-coloured amber beads our twining limbs will
    deck.'

But when that baffled Lord of War the Sun
  With gaudy pennon flying passed away
Into his brazen House, and one by one
  The little yellow stars began to stray
Across the field of heaven, ah! then indeed
She feared his lips upon her lips would never care to feed,

And cried, 'Awake, already the pale moon
  Washes the trees with silver, and the wave   410
Creeps grey and chilly up this sandy dune,
  The croaking frogs are out, and from the cave
The night-jar shrieks, the fluttering bats repass,
And the brown stoat with hollow flanks creeps through the
    dusky grass.

Nay, though thou art a God, be not so coy,
    For in yon stream there is a little reed
That often whispers how a lovely boy
    Lay with her once upon a grassy mead,
Who when his cruel pleasure he had done
Spread wings of rustling gold and soared aloft into the sun.   420

Be not so coy, the laurel trembles still
    With great Apollo's kisses, and the fir
Whose clustering sisters fringe the seaward hill
    Hath many a tale of that bold ravisher
Whom men call Boreas, and I have seen
The mocking eyes of Hermes through the poplar's silvery
      sheen.

Even the jealous Naiads call me fair,
    And every morn a young and ruddy swain
Woos me with apples and with locks of hair,
    And seeks to soothe my virginal disdain   430
By all the gifts the gentle wood-nymphs love;
But yesterday he brought to me an iris-plumaged dove

With little crimson feet, which with its store
    Of seven spotted eggs the cruel lad
Had stolen from the lofty sycamore
    At daybreak, when her amorous comrade had
Flown off in search of berried juniper
Which most they love; the fretful wasp, that earliest vintager

Of the blue grapes, hath not persistency
    So constant as this simple shepherd-boy   440
For my poor lips, his joyous purity
    And laughing sunny eyes might well decoy
A Dryad from her oath to Artemis;
For very beautiful is he, his mouth was made to kiss,

61

His argent forehead, like a rising moon
   Over the dusky hills of meeting brows,
Is crescent shaped, the hot and Tyrian noon
   Leads from the myrtle-grove no goodlier spouse
For Cytheræa, the first silky down
Fringes his blushing cheeks, and his young limbs are strong
     and brown: 450

And he is rich, and fat and fleecy herds
   Of bleating sheep upon his meadows lie,
And many an earthen bowl of yellow curds
   Is in his homestead for the thievish fly
To swim and drown in, the pink clover mead
Keeps its sweet store for him, and he can pipe on oaten reed.

And yet I love him not, it was for thee
   I kept my love, I knew that thou would'st come
To rid me of this pallid chastity;
   Thou fairest flower of the flowerless foam   460
Of all the wide Ægean, brightest star
Of ocean's azure heavens where the mirrored planets are!

I knew that thou would'st come, for when at first
   The dry wood burgeoned, and the sap of Spring
Swelled in my green and tender bark or burst
   To myriad multitudinous blossoming
Which mocked the midnight with its mimic moons
That did not dread the dawn, and first the thrushes' rapturous
     tunes

Startled the squirrel from its granary,
   And cuckoo flowers fringed the narrow lane,   470
Through my young leaves a sensuous ecstasy
   Crept like new wine, and every mossy vein
Throbbed with the fitful pulse of amorous blood,
And the wild winds of passion shook my slim stem's
     maidenhood.

The trooping fawns at evening came and laid
    Their cool black noses on my lowest boughs,
And on my topmost branch the blackbird made
    A little nest of grasses for his spouse,
And now and then a twittering wren would light
On a thin twig which hardly bare the weight of such delight.   480

I was the Attic shepherd's trysting place,
    Beneath my shadow Amaryllis lay,
And round my trunk would laughing Daphnis chase
    The timorous girl, till tired out with play
She felt his hot breath stir her tangled hair,
And turned, and looked, and fled no more from such
        delightful snare.

Then come away unto my ambuscade
    Where clustering woodbine weaves a canopy
For amorous pleasaunce, and the rustling shade
    Of Paphian myrtles seems to sanctify   490
The dearest rites of love, there in the cool
And green recesses of its farthest depth there is a pool,

The ouzel's haunt, the wild bee's pasturage,
    For round its rim great creamy lilies float
Through their flat leaves in verdant anchorage,
    Each cup a white-sailed golden-laden boat
Steered by a dragon-fly, – be not afraid
To leave this wan and wave-kissed shore, surely the place
        was made

For lovers such as we; the Cyprian Queen,
    One arm around her boyish paramour,   500
Strays often there at eve, and I have seen
    The moon strip off her misty vestiture
For young Endymion's eyes; be not afraid,
The panther feet of Dian never tread that secret glade.

Nay if thou will'st, back to the beating brine,
　　Back to the boisterous billow let us go,
And walk all day beneath the hyaline
　　Huge vault of Neptune's watery portico,
And watch the purple monsters of the deep
Sport in ungainly play, and from his lair keen Xiphias leap.　　510

For if my mistress find me lying here
　　She will not ruth or gentle pity show,
But lay her boar-spear down, and with austere
　　Relentless fingers string the cornel bow,
And draw the feathered notch against her breast,
And loose the archèd cord, ay, even now upon the quest

I hear her hurrying feet, – awake, awake,
　　Thou laggard in love's battle! once at least
Let me drink deep of passion's wine, and slake
　　My parchèd being with the nectarous feast　　520
Which even Gods affect! O come, Love, come,
Still we have time to reach the cavern of thin azure home.'

Scarce had she spoken when the shuddering trees
　　Shook, and the leaves divided, and the air
Grew conscious of a God, and the grey seas
　　Crawled backward, and a long and dismal blare
Blew from some tasselled horn, a sleuth-hound bayed,
And like a flame a barbèd reed flew whizzing down the
　　　glade.

And where the little flowers of her breast
　　Just brake into their milky blossoming,　　530
This murderous paramour, this unbidden guest,
　　Pierced and struck deep in horrid chambering,
And ploughed a bloody furrow with its dart,
And dug a long red road, and cleft with wingèd death her
　　　heart.

64

Sobbing her life out with a bitter cry
    On the boy's body fell the Dryad maid,
Sobbing for incomplete virginity,
    And raptures unenjoyed, and pleasures dead,
And all the pain of things unsatisfied,
And the bright drops of crimson youth crept down her
        throbbing side.   540

Ah! pitiful it was to hear her moan,
    And very pitiful to see her die
Ere she had yielded up her sweets, or known
    The joy of passion, that dread mystery
Which not to know is not to live at all,
And yet to know is to be held in death's most deadly thrall.

But as it hapt the Queen of Cythere,
    Who with Adonis all night long had lain
Within some shepherd's hut in Arcady,
    On team of silver doves and gilded wain   550
Was journeying Paphos-ward, high up afar
From mortal ken between the mountains and the morning
        star,

And when low down she spied the hapless pair,
    And heard the Oread's faint despairing cry,
Whose cadence seemed to play upon the air
    As though it were a viol, hastily
She bade her pigeons fold each straining plume,
And dropt to earth, and reached the strand, and saw their
        dolorous doom.

For as a gardener turning back his head
    To catch the last notes of the linnet, mows   560
With careless scythe too near some flower bed,
    And cuts the thorny pillar of the rose,
And with the flower's loosened loveliness
Strews the brown mould, or as some shepherd lad in
        wantonness

Driving his little flock along the mead
    Treads down two daffodils which side by side
Have lured the lady-bird with yellow brede
    And made the gaudy moth forget its pride,
Treads down their brimming golden chalices
Under light feet which were not made for such rude
        ravages,   570

Or as a schoolboy tired of his book
    Flings himself down upon the reedy grass
And plucks two water-lilies from the brook,
    And for a time forgets the hour glass,
Then wearies of their sweets, and goes his way,
And lets the hot sun kill them, even so these lovers lay.

And Venus cried, 'It is dread Artemis
    Whose bitter hand hath wrought this cruelty,
Or else that mightier maid whose care it is
    To guard her strong and stainless majesty   580
Upon the hill Athenian, – alas!
That they who loved so well unloved unto death's house
        should pass.

So with soft hands she laid the boy and girl
    In the great golden waggon tenderly,
Her white throat whiter than a moony pearl
    Just threaded with a blue vein's tapestry
Had not yet ceased to throb, and still her breast
Swayed like a wind-stirred lily in ambiguous unrest.

And then each pigeon spread its milky van,
    The bright car soared into the dawning sky,   590
And like a cloud the aerial caravan
    Passed over the Ægean silently,
Till the faint air was troubled with the song
From the wan mouths that call on bleeding Thammuz all
        night long.

But when the doves had reached their wonted goal
   Where the wide stair of orbèd marble dips
Its snows into the sea, her fluttering soul
   Just shook the trembling petals of her lips
And passed into the void, and Venus knew
That one fair maid the less would walk amid her retinue,   600

And bade her servants carve a cedar chest
   With all the wonder of this history,
Within whose scented womb their limbs should rest
   Where olive-trees make tender the blue sky
On the low hills of Paphos, and the faun
Pipes in the noonday, and the nightingale sings on till dawn.

Nor failed they to obey her hest, and ere
   The morning bee had stung the daffodil
With tiny fretful spear, or from its lair
   The waking stag had leapt across the rill   610
   And roused the ouzel, or the lizard crept
Athwart the sunny rock, beneath the grass their bodies slept.

And when day brake, within that silver shrine
   Fed by the flames of cressets tremulous,
Queen Venus knelt and prayed to Proserpine
   That she whose beauty made Death amorous
Should beg a guerdon from her pallid Lord,
And let Desire pass across dread Charon's icy ford.

III

In melancholy moonless Acheron,
   Far from the goodly earth and joyous day,   620
Where no spring ever buds, nor ripening sun
   Weighs down the apple trees, nor flowery May
Chequers with chestnut blooms the grassy floor,
Where thrushes never sing, and piping linnets mate no more,

There by a dim and dark Lethæan well
    Young Charmides was lying, wearily
He plucked the blossoms from the asphodel,
    And with its little rifled treasury
Strewed the dull waters of the dusky stream,
And watched the white stars founder, and the land was
      like a dream,   630

When as he gazed into the watery glass
    And through his brown hair's curly tangles scanned
His own wan face, a shadow seemed to pass
    Across the mirror, and a little hand
Stole into his, and warm lips timidly
Brushed his pale cheeks, and breathed their secret forth
      into a sigh.

Then turned he round his weary eyes and saw,
    And ever nigher still their faces came,
And nigher ever did their young mouths draw
    Until they seemed one perfect rose of flame,   640
And longing arms around her neck he cast,
And felt her throbbing bosom, and his breath came hot and
      fast,

And all his hoarded sweets were hers to kiss,
    And all her maidenhood was his to slay,
And limb to limb in long and rapturous bliss
    Their passion waxed and waned, – O why essay
To pipe again of love, too venturous reed!
Enough, enough that Erôs laughed upon that flowerless mead.

Too venturous poesy, O why essay
    To pipe again of passion! fold thy wings   650
O'er daring Icarus and bid thy lay
    Sleep hidden in the lyre's silent strings
Till thou hast found the old Castalian rill,
Or from the Lesbian waters plucked drowned Sappho's
      golden quill!

Enough, enough that he whose life had been
   A fiery pulse of sin, a splendid shame,
Could in the loveless land of Hades glean
   One scorching harvest from those fields of flame
Where passion walks with naked unshod feet
And is not wounded, – ah! enough that once their lips could
      meet   660

In that wild throb when all existences
   Seemed narrowed to one single ecstasy
Which dies through its own sweetness and the stress
   Of too much pleasure, ere Persephone
Had bade them serve her by the ebon throne
Of the pale God who in the fields of Enna loosed her zone.

Impression de Voyage

The sea was sapphire coloured, and the sky
   Burned like a heated opal through the air;
   We hoisted sail; the wind was blowing fair
For the blue lands that to the eastward lie.
From the steep prow I marked with quickening eye
   Zakynthos, every olive grove and creek,
   Ithaca's cliff, Lycaon's snowy peak,
And all the flower-strewn hills of Arcady.
The flapping of the sail against the mast,
   The ripple of the water on the side,
   The ripple of girls' laughter at the stern,
The only sounds: – when 'gan the West to burn,
   And a red sun upon the seas to ride,
   I stood upon the soil of Greece at last!

Katakolo

Portia

To Ellen Terry

I marvel not Bassanio was so bold
   To peril all he had upon the lead,
   Or that proud Aragon bent low his head
Or that Morocco's fiery heart grew cold:
For in that gorgeous dress of beaten gold
   Which is more golden than the golden sun
   No woman Veronesé looked upon
Was half so fair as thou whom I behold.
Yet fairer when with wisdom as your shield
   The sober-suited lawyer's gown you donned,
And would not let the laws of Venice yield
   Antonio's heart to that accursèd Jew –
   O Portia! take my heart: it is thy due:
I think I will not quarrel with the Bond.

Camma

As one who poring on a Grecian urn
   Scans the fair shapes some Attic hand hath made,
   God with slim goddess, goodly man with maid,
And for their beauty's sake is loth to turn
And face the obvious day, must I not yearn
   For many a secret moon of indolent bliss,
   When in the midmost shrine of Artemis
I see thee standing, antique-limbed, and stern?

And yet – methinks I'd rather see thee play
   That serpent of old Nile, whose witchery
Made Emperors drunken, – come, great Egypt, shake
   Our stage with all thy mimic pageants! Nay,
   I am grown sick of unreal passions, make
The world thine Actium, me thine Anthony!

Panthea

Nay, let us walk from fire unto fire,
   ·From passionate pain to deadlier delight, –
I am too young to live without desire,
   Too young art thou to waste this summer night
Asking those idle questions which of old
Man sought of seer and oracle, and no reply was told.

For, sweet, to feel is better than to know,
   And wisdom is a childless heritage,
One pulse of passion – youth's first fiery glow, –
   Are worth the hoarded proverbs of the sage: 10
Vex not thy soul with dead philosophy,
   Have we not lips to kiss with, hearts to love and eyes to see!

Dost thou not hear the murmuring nightingale,
   Like water bubbling from a silver jar,
So soft she sings the envious moon is pale,
   That high in heaven she is hung so far
She cannot hear that love-enraptured tune, –
Mark how she wreathes each horn with mist, yon late and
     labouring moon.

White lilies, in whose cups the gold bees dream,
   The fallen snow of petals where the breeze   20
Scatters the chestnut blossom, or the gleam
   Of boyish limbs in water, – are not these
Enough for thee, dost thou desire more?
Alas! the Gods will give nought else from their eternal store.

For our high Gods have sick and wearied grown
   Of all our endless sins, our vain endeavour
For wasted days of youth to make atone
   By pain or prayer or priest, and never, never,
Hearken they now to either good or ill,
But send their rain upon the just and the unjust at will.   30

They sit at ease, our Gods they sit at ease,
    Strewing with leaves of rose their scented wine,
They sleep, they sleep, beneath the rocking trees
    Where asphodel and yellow lotus twine,
Mourning the old glad days before they knew
What evil things the heart of man could dream, and
        dreaming do.

And far beneath the brazen floor they see
    Like swarming flies the crowd of little men,
The bustle of small lives, then wearily
    Back to their lotus-haunts they turn again   40
Kissing each others' mouths, and mix more deep
The poppy-seeded draught which brings soft purple-lidded
        sleep.

There all day long the golden-vestured sun,
    Their torch-bearer, stands with his torch ablaze,
And, when the gaudy web of noon is spun
    By its twelve maidens, through the crimson haze
Fresh from Endymion's arms comes forth the moon,
    And the immortal Gods in toils of mortal passions swoon.

There walks Queen Juno through some dewy mead,
    Her grand white feet flecked with the saffron dust   50
Of wind-stirred lilies, while young Ganymede
    Leaps in the hot and amber-foaming must,
His curls all tossed, as when the eagle bare
The frightened boy from Ida through the blue Ionian air.

There in the green heart of some garden close
    Queen Venus with the shepherd at her side,
Her warm soft body like the briar rose
    Which would be white yet bluishes at its pride,
Laughs low for love, till jealous Salmacis
Peers through the myrtle-leaves and sighs for pain of
        lonely bliss.   60

72

There never does that dreary north-wind blow
    Which leaves our English forests bleak and bare,
Nor ever falls the swift white-feathered snow,
    Nor ever doth the red-toothed lightning dare
To wake them in the silver-fretted night
When we lie weeping for some sweet sad sin, some dead
        delight.

Alas! they know the far Lethæan spring,
    The violet-hidden waters well they know,
Where one whose feet with tired wandering
    Are faint and broken may take heart and go,   70
And from those dark depths cool and crystalline
Drink, and draw balm, and sleep for sleepless souls, and
        anodyne.

But we oppress our natures, God or Fate
    Is our enemy, we starve and feed
On vain repentance – O we are born too late!
    What balm for us in bruisèd poppy seed
Who crowd into one finite pulse of time
The joy of infinite love and the fierce pain of infinite crime.

O we are wearied of this sense of guilt,
    Wearied of pleasure's paramour despair,   80
Wearied of every temple we have built,
    Wearied of every right, unanswered prayer,
For man is weak; God sleeps: and heaven is high:
One fiery-coloured moment: one great love; and lo! we die.

Ah! but no ferry-man with labouring pole
    Nears his black shallop to the flowerless strand,
No little coin of bronze can bring the soul
    Over Death's river to the sunless land,
Victim and wine and vow are all in vain,
The tomb is sealed; the soldiers watch; the dead rise not
        again.   90

73

We are resolved into the supreme air,
    We are made one with what we touch and see,
With our heart's blood each crimson sun is fair,
    With our young lives each spring-impassioned tree
Flames into green, the wildest beasts that range
The moor our kinsmen are, all life is one, and all is change.

With beat of systole and of diastole
    One grand great life throbs through earth's giant heart,
And mighty waves of single Being roll
    From nerveless germ to man, for we are part   100
Of every rock and bird and beast and hill,
One with the things that prey on us, and one with what we
        kill.

From lower cells of waking life we pass
    To full perfection; thus the world grows old:
We who are godlike now were once a mass
    Of quivering purple flecked with bars of gold,
Unsentient or of joy or misery,
And tossed in terrible tangles of some wild and wind-swept
        sea.

This hot hard flame with which our bodies burn
    Will make some meadow blaze with daffodil,   110
Ay! and those argent beasts of thine will turn
    To water-lilies; the brown fields men till
Will be more fruitful for our love to-night,
Nothing is lost in nature, all things live in Death's despite.

The boy's first kiss, the hyacinth's first bell,
    The man's last passion, and the last red spear
That from the lily leaps, the asphodel
    Which will not let its blossoms blow for fear
Of too much beauty, and the timid shame
Of the young bridegroom at his lover's eyes, – these with
        the same   120

One sacrament are consecrate, the earth
    Not we alone hath passions hymeneal,
The yellow buttercups that shake for mirth
    At daybreak know a pleasure not less real
Than we do, when in some fresh-blossoming wood,
We draw the spring into our hearts, and feel that life is good.

So when men bury us beneath the yew
    Thy crimson-stainèd mouth a rose will be,
And thy soft eyes lush bluebells dimmed with dew,
    And when the white narcissus wantonly   130
Kisses the wind its playmate some faint joy
Will thrill our dust, and we will be again fond maid and boy.

And thus without life's conscious torturing pain
    In some sweet flower we will feel the sun,
And from the linnet's throat will sing again,
    And as two gorgeous-mailèd snakes will run
Over our graves, or as two tigers creep
Through the hot jungle where the yellow-eyed huge lions
        sleep

And give them battle! How my heart leaps up
    To think of that grand living after death   140
In beast and bird and flower, when this cup,
    Being filled too full of spirit, bursts for breath,
And with the pale leaves of some autumn day
The soul earth's earliest conqueror becomes earth's last great
        prey.

O think of it! We shall inform ourselves
    Into all sensuous life, the goat-foot Faun,
The Centaur, or the merry bright-eyed Elves
    That leave their dancing rings to spite the dawn
Upon the meadows, shall not be more near
Than you and I to nature's mysteries, for we shall hear   150

The thrush's heart beat, and the daisies grow,
  And the wan snowdrop sighing for the sun
On sunless days in winter, we shall know
  By whom the silver gossamer is spun,
Who paints the diapered fritillaries,
On what wide wings from shivering pine to pine the eagle
    flies.

Ay! had we never loved at all, who knows
  If yonder daffodil had lured the bee
Into its gilded womb, or any rose
  Had hung with crimson lamps its little tree!   160
Methinks no leaf would ever bud in spring,
But for the lovers' lips that kiss, the poets' lips that sing.

Is the light vanished from our golden sun,
  Or is this dædal-fashioned earth less fair,
That we are nature's heritors, and one
  With every pulse of life that beats the air?
Rather new suns across the sky shall pass,
New splendour come unto the flower, new glory to the grass.

And we two lovers shall not sit afar,
  Critics of nature, but the joyous sea   170
Shall be our raiment, and the bearded star
  Shoot arrows at our pleasure! We shall be
Part of the mighty universal whole,
And through all æons mix and mingle with the Kosmic Soul!

We shall be notes in that great Symphony
  Whose cadence circles through the rhythmic spheres,
And all the live World's throbbing heart shall be
  One with our heart, the stealthy creeping years
Have lost their terrors now, we shall not die,
The Universe itself shall be our Immortality!   180

76

Impression
Le Réveillon

The sky is laced with fitful red,
  The circling mists and shadows flee,
  The dawn is rising from the sea,
Like a white lady from her bed.

And jagged brazen arrows fall
  Athwart the feathers of the night,
  And a long wave of yellow light
Breaks silently on tower and hall,

And spreading wide across the wold
  Wakes into flight some fluttering bird,
  And all the chestnut tops are stirred,
And all the branches streaked with gold.

Quia Multum Amavi

Dear Heart, I think the young impassioned priest
  When first he takes from out the hidden shrine
His God imprisoned in the Eucharist,
  And eats the bread, and drinks the dreadful wine,

Feels not such awful wonder as I felt
  When first my smitten eyes beat full on thee,
And all night long before thy feet I knelt
  Till thou wert wearied of Idolatry.

Ah! hadst thou liked me less and loved me more,
  Through all those summer days of joy and rain,
I had not now been sorrow's heritor,
  Or stood a lackey in the House of Pain.

Yet, though remorse, youth's white-faced seneschal,
　　Tread on my heels with all his retinue,
I am most glad I loved thee – think of all
　　The suns that go to make one speedwell blue!

Silentium Amoris

As often-times the too resplendent sun
　　Hurries the pallid and reluctant moon
Back to her sombre cave, ere she hath won
　　A single ballad from the nightingale,
　　So doth my Beauty make my lips to fail,
And all my sweetest singing out of tune.

And as at dawn across the level mead
　　On wings impetuous some wind will come,
And with its too harsh kisses break the reed
　　Which was its only instrument of song,
　　So my too stormy passions work me wrong,
And for excess of Love my Love is dumb.

But surely unto Thee mine eyes did show
　　Why I am silent, and my lute unstrung;
Else it were better we should part, and go,
　　Thou to some lips of sweeter melody,
　　And I to nurse the barren memory
Of unkissed kisses, and songs never sung.

Her Voice

The wild bee reels from bough to bough
  With his furry coat and his gauzy wing,
Now in a lily-cup, and now
  Setting a jacinth bell a-swing,
    In his wandering;
Sit closer love: it was here I trow
  I made that vow,

Swore that two lives should be like one
  As long as the sea-gull loved the sea,
As long as the sunflower sought the sun, –
  It shall be, I said, for eternity
    'Twixt you and me!
Dear friend, those times are over and done,
  Love's web is spun.

Look upward where the poplar trees
  Sway and sway in the summer air,
Here in the valley never a breeze
  Scatters the thistledown, but there
    Great winds blow fair
From the mighty murmuring mystical seas,
  And the wave-lashed leas.

Look upward where the white gull screams,
  What does it see that we do not see?
Is that a star? or the lamp that gleams
  On some outward voyaging argosy, –
    Ah! can it be
We have lived our lives in a land of dreams!
  How sad it seems.

Sweet, there is nothing left to say
  But this, that love is never lost,
Keen winter stabs the breasts of May
  Whose crimson roses burst his frost,

            Ships tempest-tossed
        Will find a harbour in some bay,
            And so we may.

        And there is nothing left to do
            But to kiss once again, and part,
        Nay, there is nothing we should rue,
            I have my beauty, – you your Art,
                Nay, do not start,
        One world was not enough for two
            Like me and you.

                    My Voice

    Within this restless, hurried, modern world
        We took our hearts' full pleasure – You and I,
    And now the white sails of our ships are furled,
        And spent the lading of our argosy.

    Wherefore my cheeks before their time are wan,
        For very weeping is my gladness fled,
    Sorrow has paled my young mouth's vermilion,
        And Ruin draws the curtains of my bed.

    But all this crowded life has been to thee
        No more than lyre, or lute, or subtle spell
    Of viols, or the music of the sea
        That sleeps, a mimic echo, in the shell.

from *Humanitad*

It is full winter now: the trees are bare,
  Save where the cattle huddle from the cold
Beneath the pine, for it doth never wear
  The Autumn's gaudy livery whose gold
Her jealous brother pilfers, but is true
To the green doublet; bitter is the wind, as though it blew

From Saturn's cave; a few thin wisps of hay
  Lie on the sharp black hedges, where the wain
Dragged the sweet pillage of a summer's day
  From the low meadows up the narrow lane;   10
Upon the half-thawed snow the bleating sheep
Press close against the hurdles, and the shivering house-dogs
    creep

From the shut stable to the frozen stream
  And back again disconsolate, and miss
The bawling shepherds and the noisy team;
  And overhead in circling listlessness
The cawing rooks whirl round the frosted stack,
Or crowd the dripping boughs; and in the fen the ice-pools
    crack

Where the gaunt bittern stalks among the reeds
  And flaps his wings, and stretches back his neck,   20
And hoots to see the moon; across the meads
  Limps the poor frightened hare, a little speck;
And a stray seamew with its fretful cry
Flits like a sudden drift of snow against the dull grey sky.

ΓΛΥΚΥΠΙΚΡΟΣ ΕΡΩΣ

Flower of Love

Sweet, I blame you not, for mine the fault was, had I not
  been made of common clay
I had climbed the higher heights unclimbed yet, seen the
  fuller air, the larger day.

From the wildness of my wasted passion I had struck a
  better, clearer song,
Lit some lighter light of freer freedom, battled with some
  Hydra-headed wrong.

Had my lips been smitten into music by the kisses that but
  made them bleed,
You had walked with Bice and the angels on that verdant
  and enamelled mead.

I had trod the road which Dante treading saw the suns of
  seven circles shine,
Ay! perchance had seen the heavens opening, as they
  opened to the Florentine.

And the mighty nations would have crowned me, who am
  crownless now and without name,
And some orient dawn had found me kneeling on the
  threshold of the House of Fame.   10

I had sat within that marble circle where the oldest bard is
  as the young,
And the pipe is ever dropping honey, and the lyre's strings
  are ever strung.

Keats had lifted up his hymeneal curls from out the poppy-
  seeded wine,
With ambrosial mouth had kissed my forehead, clasped
  the hand of noble love in mine.

82

And at springtide, when the apple-blossoms brush the
    burnished bosom of the dove,
Two young lovers lying in an orchard would have read the
    story of our love.

Would have read the legend of my passion, known the
    bitter secret of my heart,
Kissed as we have kissed, but never parted as we two are
    fated now to part.

For the crimson flower of our life is eaten by the cankerworm
    of truth,
And no hand can gather up the fallen withered petals of
    the rose of youth.   20

Yet I am not sorry that I loved you – ah! what else had I a boy
    to do, –
For the hungry teeth of time devour, and the silent-footed
    years pursue.

Rudderless, we drifth athwart a tempest, and when once
    the storm of youth is past,
Without lyre, without lute or chorus, Death the silent pilot
    comes at last.

And within the grave there is no pleasure, for the blind-
    worm battens on the root,
And Desire shudders into ashes, and the tree of Passion
    bears no fruit.

Ah! what else had I to do but love you, God's own mother
    was less dear to me,
And less dear the Cytheræan rising like an argent lily from
    the sea.

I have made my choice, have lived my poems, and, though
    youth is gone in wasted days,
I have found the lover's crown of myrtle better than the
    poet's crown of bays.   30

Impressions

I

Le Jardin

The lily's withered chalice falls
   Around its rod of dusty gold,
   And from the beech-trees on the wold
The last wood-pigeon coos and calls.

The gaudy leonine sunflower
   Hangs black and barren on its stalk,
   And down the windy garden walk
The dead leaves scatter, – hour by hour.

Pale privet-petals white as milk
   Are blown into a snowy mass:
   The roses lie upon the grass
Like little shreds of crimson silk.

II

La Mer

A white mist drifts across the shrouds
   A wild moon in this wintry sky
   Gleams like an angry lion's eye
Out of a mane of tawny clouds.

The muffled steersman at the wheel
   Is but a shadow in the gloom; –
   And in the throbbing engine room
Leap the long rods of polished steel.

The shattered storm has left its trace
   Upon this huge and heaving dome,
   For the thin threads of yellow foam
Float on the waves like ravelled lace.

The Harlot's House

We caught the tread of dancing feet,
We loitered down the moonlit street,
And stopped beneath the harlot's house.

Inside, above the din and fray,
We heard the loud musicians play
The 'Treues Liebes Herz' of Strauss.

Like strange mechanical grotesques,
Making fantastic arabesques,
The shadows raced across the blind.

We watched the ghostly dancers spin   10
To sound of horn and violin,
Like black leaves wheeling in the wind.

Like wire-pulled automatons,
Slim silhouetted skeletons
Went sidling through the slow quadrille.

They took each other by the hand,
And danced a stately saraband;
Their laughter echoed thin and shrill.

Sometimes a clockwork puppet pressed
A phantom lover to her breast,   20
Sometimes they seemed to try to sing.

Sometimes a horrible marionette
Came out, and smoked its cigarette
Upon the steps like a live thing.

Then, turning to my love, I said,
'The dead are dancing with the dead,
The dust is whirling with the dust.'

But she – she heard the violin,
And left my side, and entered in:
Love passed into the house of lust.   30

Then suddenly the tune went false,
The dancers wearied of the waltz,
The shadows ceased to wheel and whirl.

And down the long and silent street,
The dawn, with silver-sandalled feet,
Crept like a frightened girl.

On the Sale by Auction of Keats' Love Letters

These are the letters which Endymion wrote
    To one he loved in secret, and apart.
    And now the brawlers of the auction mart
Bargain and bid for each poor blotted note,
Ay! for each separate pulse of passion quote
    The merchant's price. I think they love not art
    Who break the crystal of a poet's heart
That small and sickly eyes may glare and gloat.

Is it not said that many years ago,
    In a far Eastern town, some soldiers ran
    With torches through the midnight, and began
To wrangle for mean raiment, and to throw
    Dice for the garments of a wretched man,
Not knowing the God's wonder, or His woe?

Les Ballons

Against these turbid turquoise skies
  The light and luminous ballons
  Dip and drift like satin moons,
Drift like silken butterflies;

Reel with every windy gust,
  Rise and reel like dancing girls,
  Float like strange transparent pearls,
Fall and float like silver dust.

Now to the low leaves they cling,
  Each with coy fantastic pose,
  Each a petal of a rose
Straining at a gossamer string.

Then to the tall trees they climb,
  Like thin globes of amethyst,
  Wandering opals keeping tryst
With the rubies of the lime.

Symphony in Yellow

An omnibus across the bridge
  Crawls like a yellow butterfly,
  And, here and there, a passer-by
Shows like a little restless midge.

Big barges full of yellow hay
  Are moved against the shadowy wharf,
  And, like a yellow silken scarf,
The thick fog hangs along the quay.

The yellow leaves begin to fade
   And flutter from the Temple elms,
   And at my feet the pale green Thames
Lies like a rod of rippled jade.

To My Wife
with a copy of my poems

I can write no stately proem
   As a prelude to my lay;
From a poet to a poem
   I would dare to say.

For if of these fallen petals
   One to you seem fair,
Love will waft it till it settles
   On your hair.

And when wind and winter harden
   All the loveless land,
It will whisper of the garden,
   You will understand.

To L.L.

Could we dig up this long-buried treasure,
   Were it worth the pleasure,
We never could learn love's song,
   We are parted too long.

Could the passionate past that is fled
   Call back its dead,
Could we live it all over again,
   Were it worth the pain!

I remember we used to meet
    By an ivied seat,   10
And you warbled each pretty word
    With the air of a bird;

And your voice had a quaver in it,
    Just like a linnet,
And shook, as the blackbird's throat
    With its last big note;

And your eyes, they were green and grey
    Like an April day,
But lit into amethyst
    When I stooped and kissed;   20

And your mouth, it would never smile
    For a long, long while,
Then it rippled all over with laughter
    Five minutes after.

You were always afraid of a shower,
    Just like a flower:
I remember you started and ran
    When the rain began.

I remember I never could catch you,
    For no one could match you,   30
You had wonderful, luminous, fleet,
    Little wings to your feet.

I remember your hair – did I tie it?
    For it always ran riot –
Like a tangled sunbeam of gold:
    These things are old.

I remember so well the room,
    And the lilac bloom
That beat at the dripping pane
    In the warm June rain;   40

And the colour of your gown,
    It was amber-brown,
And two yellow satin bows
    From your shoulders rose.

And the handkerchief of French lace
    Which you held to your face –
Had a small tear left a stain?
    Or was it the rain?

On your hand as it waved adieu
    There were veins of blue;   50
In your voice as it said good-bye
    Was a petulant cry,

'You have only wasted your life.'
    (Ah, that was the knife!)
When I rushed through the garden gate
    It was all too late.

Could we live it over again,
    Were it worth the pain,
Could the passionate past that is fled
    Call back its dead!   60

Well, if my heart must break,
    Dear love, for your sake,
It will break in music, I know,
    Poets' hearts break so.

But strange that I was not told
    That the brain can hold
In a tiny ivory cell
    God's heaven and hell.

from *Ravenna*

Newdigate Prize Poem
Recited in the Sheldonian Theatre
Oxford
26 June 1878

IV

How lone this palace is; how grey the walls!
No minstrel now wakes echoes in these halls.
The broken chain lies rusting on the door,
And noisome weeds have split the marble floor: 110
Here lurks the snake, and here the lizards run
By the stone lions blinking in the sun.
Byron dwelt here in love and revelry
For two long years – a second Anthony,
Who of the world another Actium made!
Yet suffered not his royal soul to fade,
Or lyre to break, or lance to grow less keen,
'Neath any wiles of an Egyptian queen.
For from the East there came a mighty cry,
And Greece stood up to fight for Liberty,   120
And called him from Ravenna: never knight
Rode forth more nobly to wild scenes of fight!
None fell more bravely on ensanguined field,
Borne like a Spartan back upon his shield!
O Hellas! Hellas! in thine hour of pride,
Thy day of might, remember him who died
To wrest from off thy limbs the trammelling chain:
O Salamis! O lone Platæan plain!
O tossing waves of wild Eubœan sea!
O wind-swept heights of lone Thermopylæ!   130
He loved you well – ay, not alone in word,
Who freely gave to thee his lyre and sword,
Like Æschylos at well-fought Marathon:

And England, too, shall glory in her son,
Her warrior-poet, first in song and fight.
No longer now shall Slander's venomed spite
Crawl like a snake across his perfect name,
Or mar the lordly scutcheon of his fame.

For as the olive-garland of the race,
Which lights with joy each eager runner's face,   140
As the red cross which saveth men in war,
As a flame-bearded beacon seen from far
By mariners upon a storm-tossed sea, –
Such was his love for Greece and Liberty!

Byron, thy crowns are ever fresh and green:
Red leaves of rose from Sapphic Mitylene
Shall bind thy brows; the myrtle blooms for thee,
In hidden glades by lonely Castaly;
The laurels wait thy coming: all are thine,
And round thy head one perfect wreath will twine.   150

V

The pine-tops rocked before the evening breeze
With the hoarse murmur of the wintry seas,
And the tall stems were streaked with amber bright; –
I wandered through the wood in wild delight,
Some startled bird, with fluttering wings and fleet,
Made snow of all the blossoms; at my feet,
Like silver crowns, the pale narcissi lay,
And small birds sang on every twining spray.
O waving trees, O forest liberty!
Within your haunts at least a man is free,   160
And half forgets the weary world of strife:
The blood flows hotter, and a sense of life
Wakes i' the quickening veins, while once again
The woods are filled with gods we fancied slain.
Long time I watched, and surely hoped to see

Some goat-foot Pan make merry minstrelsy
Amid the reeds! some startled Dryad-maid
In girlish flight! or lurking in the glade,
The soft brown limbs, the wanton treacherous face
Of woodland god! Queen Dian in the chase,   170
White-limbed and terrible, with look of pride,
And leash of boar-hounds leaping at her side!
Or Hylas mirrored in the perfect stream.

O idle heart! O fond Hellenic dream!
Ere long, with melancholy rise and swell,
The evening chimes, the convent's vesper-bell,
Struck on mine ears amid the amorous flowers.
Alas! alas! these sweet and honied hours   180
Had whelmed my heart like some encroaching sea,
And drowned all thoughts of black Gethsemane.

from *Chorus of Cloud Maidens*
(Ἀριστοφανους Νεφέλαι, 275-290)

ΣΤΡΟΦΗ

Cloud maidens that float on for ever,
    Dew-sprinkled, fleet bodies, and fair,
Let us rise from our Sire's loud river,
    Great Ocean, and soar through the air
To the peaks of the pine-covered mountains where the pines
            hang as tresses of hair.
Let us seek the watch-towers undaunted,
    Where the well-watered corn-fields abound,
And through murmurs of rivers nymph-haunted
    The songs of the sea-waves resound;
And the sun in the sky never wearies of spreading his radiance
            around.

Let us cast off the haze
　　Of the mists from our band,
Till with far-seeing gaze
　　We may look on the land.

from ΘΡΗΝΩΙΔΙΑ
(Eur. Hec., 11.444ff.)

Song sung by captive women of Troy on the sea beach at Aulis, while
the Achæans were there storm-bound through the wrath of dishonoured
Achilles, and waiting for a fair wind to bring them home.

ΣΤΡΟΦΗ

O fair wind blowing from the sea!
　　Who through the dark and mist dost guide
　　The ships that on the billows ride
Unto what land, ah, misery!
Shall I be borne, across what stormy wave,
Or to whose house a purchased slave?

O sea-wind blowing fair and fast
　　Is it unto the Dorian strand,
　　　Or to those far and fable shores,
　　　Where great Apidanus outpours   10
　　His streams upon the fertile land,
　　Or shall I tread the Phthian sand,
Borne by the swift breath of the blast?

ΑΝΤΙΣΤΡΟΦΗ

O blowing wind! you bring my sorrow near,
　　For surely borne with splashing of the oar,
And hidden in some galley-prison drear
　　I shall be lead unto that distant shore

94

Where the tall palm-tree first took root, and made,
With clustering laurel leaves, a pleasant shade
For Leto when with travail great she bore   20
A god and goddess in Love's bitter fight,
Her body's anguish, and her soul's delight.

It may be in Delos,
   Encircled of seas,
I shall sing with some maids
   From the Cyclades,
Of Artemis goddess
   And queen and maiden,
Sing of the gold
   In her hair heavy-laden.   30
Sing of her hunting,
   Her arrows and bow,
And in singing find solace
   From weeping and woe.

The Sphinx

In a dim corner of my room for longer than my fancy thinks
A beautiful and silent Sphinx has watched me through the
    shifting gloom.

Inviolate and immobile she does not rise she does not stir
For silver moons are naught to her and naught to her the
    suns that reel.

Red follows grey across the air the waves of moonlight ebb
    and flow
But with the Dawn she does not go and in the night-time
    she is there.

Upon the mat she lies and leers and on the tawny throat of
    her
Flutters the soft and silky fur or ripples to her pointed ears.   10

Come forth, my lovely seneschal! so somnolent, so
    statuesque!
Come forth you exquisite grotesque! half woman and half
    animal!

Come forth my lovely languorous Sphinx! and put your
    head upon my knee!
And let me stroke your throat and see your body spotted
    like the Lynx!

And let me touch those curving claws of yellow ivory and
    grasp
The tail that like a monstrous Asp coils round your heavy
    velvet paws!

                              *

A thousand weary centuries are thine while I have hardly
    seen
Some twenty summers cast their green for Autumn's gaudy
    liveries.

But you can read the Hieroglyphs on the great sandstone
    obelisks,
And you have talked with Basilisks, and you have looked
    on Hippogriffs.   20

O tell me, were you standing by when Isis to Osiris knelt?
And did you watch the Egyptian melt her union for Antony

And drink the jewel-drunken wine and bend her head in
    mimic awe
To see the huge proconsul draw the salted tunny from the
    brine?

And did you mark the Cyprian kiss white Adon on his
    catafalque?
And did you follow Amenalk, the God of Heliopolis?

And did you talk with Thoth, and did you hear the moon-
    horned Io weep?
And know the painted kings who sleep beneath the wedge-
    shaped Pyramid?

*

Lift up your large black satin eyes which are like cushions
    where one sinks!
Fawn at my feet, fantastic Sphinx! and sing me all your
    memories!   30

Sing to me of the Jewish maid who wandered with the Holy
    Child,
And how you led them through the wild, and how they
    slept beneath your shade.

Sing to me of that odorous green eve when couching by
    the marge
You heard from Adrian's gilded barge the laughter of
    Antinous

And lapped the stream and fed your drouth and watched
    with hot and hungry stare
The ivory body of that rare young slave with his
    pomegranate mouth!

Sing to me of the Labyrinth in which the twi-formed bull
    was stalled!
Sing to me of the night you crawled across the temple's
    granite plinth

When through the purple corridors the screaming scarlet
    Ibis flew

In terror, and a horrid dew dripped from the moaning
    Mandragores,   40

And the great torpid crocodile within the tank shed slimy
    tears,
And tare the jewels from his ears and staggered back into
    the Nile,

And the priests cursed you with shrill psalms as in your
    claws you seized their snake
And crept away with it to slake your passion by the
    shuddering palms.

*

Who were your lovers? who were they who wrestled for
    you in the dust?
Which was the vessel of your Lust? What Leman had you,
    every day?

Did giant Lizards come and crouch before you on the reedy
    banks?
Did Gryphons with great metal flanks leap on you in your
    trampled couch?

Did monstrous hippopotami come sidling toward you in
    the mist?
Did gilt-scaled dragons writhe and twist with passion as
    you passed them by?   50

And from the brick-built Lycian tomb what horrible Chimera
    came
With fearful heads and fearful flame to breed new wonders
    from your womb?

*

Or had you shameful secret quests and did you harry to your home
Some Nereid coiled in amber foam with curious rock crystal breasts?

Or did you treading through the froth call to the brown Sidonian
For tidings of Leviathan, Leviathan or Behemoth?

Or did you when the sun was set climb up the cactus-covered slope
To meet your swarthy Ethiop whose body was of polished jet?

Or did you while the earthen skiffs dropped down the grey Nilotic flats
At twilight and the flickering bats flew round the temple's triple glyphs   60

Steal to the border of the bar and swim across the silent lake
And slink into the vault and make the Pyramid your lúpanar

Till from each black sarcophagus rose up the painted swathèd dead?
Or did you lure unto your bed the ivory-horned Tragelaphos?

Or did you love the god of flies who plagued the Hebrews and was splashed
With wine unto the waist? or Pasht, who had green beryls for her eyes?

Or that young god, the Tyrian, who was more amorous than the dove
Of Ashtaroth? or did you love the god of the Assyrian

Whose wings, like strange transparent talc, rose high above his hawk-faced head,

99

Painted with silver and with red and ribbed with rods of
    Oreichalch?   70

Or did huge Apis from his car leap down and lay before
    your feet
Big blossoms of the honey-sweet and honey-coloured
    nenuphar?

                      *

How subtle-secret is your smile! Did you love none then?
    Nay, I know
Great Ammon was your bedfellow! He lay with you beside
    the Nile!

The river-horses in the slime trumpeted when they saw
    him come
Odorous with Syrian galbanum and smeared with spikenard
    and with thyme.

He came along the river bank like some tall galley argent-
    sailed,
He strode across the waters, mailed in beauty, and the
    waters sank.

He strode across the desert sand: he reached the valley
    where you lay:
He waited till the dawn of day: then touched your black
    breasts with his hand.   80

You kissed his mouth with mouths of flame: you made the
    hornèd god your own:
You stood behind him on his throne: you called him by his
    secret name.

You whispered monstrous oracles into the caverns of his ears:
With blood of goats and blood of steers you taught him
    monstrous miracles.

White Ammon was your bedfellow! Your chamber was the
    steaming Nile!
And with your curved archaic smile you watched his
    passion come and go.

*

With Syrian oils his brows were bright: and wide-spread
    as a tent at noon
His marble limbs made pale the moon and lent the day a
    larger light.

His long hair was nine cubits' span and coloured like that
    yellow gem
Which hidden in their garment's hem the merchants bring
    from Kurdistan.   90

His face was as the must that lies upon a vat of new-made
    wine:
The seas could not insapphirine the perfect azure of his eyes.

His thick soft throat was white as milk and threaded with
    the veins of blue:
And curious pearls like frozen dew were broidered on his
    flowing silk.

*

On pearl and porphyry pedestalled he was too bright to
    look upon:
For on his ivory breast there shone the wondrous ocean-
    emerald,

That mystic moonlit jewel which some diver of the Colchian
    caves
Had found beneath the blackening waves and carried to
    the Colchian witch.

101

Before his gilded galiot ran naked vine-wreathed corybants,
And lines of swaying elephants knelt down to draw his
    chariot,   100

And lines of swarthy Nubians bare up his litter as he rode
Down the great granite-paven road between the nodding
    peacock-fans.

The merchants brought him steatite from Sidon in their
    painted ships:
The meanest cup that touched his lips was fashioned from
    a chrysolite.

The merchants brought him cedar chests of rich apparel
    bound with cords:
His train was borne by Memphian lords: young kings were
    glad to be his guests.

Ten hundred shaven priests did bow to Ammon's altar day
    and night,
Ten hundred lamps did wave their light through Ammon's
    carven house – and now

Foul snake and speckled adder with their young ones
    crawl from stone to stone
For ruined is the house and prone the great rose-marble
    monolith!   110

Wild ass or trotting jackal comes and couches in the
    mouldering gates:
Wild satyrs call unto their mates across the fallen fluted
    drums.

And on the summit of the pile the blue-faced ape of Horus
    sits
And gibbers while the fig-tree splits the pillars of the peristyle.

*

The god is scattered here and there: deep hidden in the
    windy sand
I saw his giant granite hand still clenched in impotent
    despair.

And many a wandering caravan of stately negroes silken-
    shawled,
Crossing the desert, halts appalled before the neck that
    none can span.

And many a bearded Bedouin draws back his yellow-
    striped burnous
To gaze upon the Titan thews of him who was thy paladin.   120

*

Go, seek his fragments on the moor and wash them in the
    evening dew,
And from their pieces make anew thy mutilated paramour!

Go, seek them where they lie alone and from their broken
    pieces make
Thy bruisèd bedfellow! And wake mad passions in the
    senseless stone!

Charm his dull ear with Syrian hymns! he loved your body!
    oh, be kind,
Pour spikenard on his hair, and wind soft rolls of linen
    round his limbs!

Wind round his head the figured coins! stain with red
    fruits those pallid lips!
Weave purple for his shrunken hips! and purple for his
    barren loins!

*

Away to Egypt! Have no fear. Only one God has ever died.
Only one God has let His side be wounded by a soldier's
    spear.   130

But these, thy lovers, are not dead. Still by the hundred-
    cubit gate
Dog-faced Anubis sits in state with lotus-lilies for thy head.

Still from his chair of porphyry gaunt Memnon strains his
    lidless eyes
Across the empty land, and cries each yellow morning unto
    thee.

And Nilus with his broken horn lies in his black and oozy
    bed
And till thy coming will not spread his waters on the withering
    corn.

Your lovers are not dead, I know. They will rise up and hear
    your voice
And clash their cymbals and rejoice and run to kiss your
    mouth! And so,

Set wings upon your argosies! Set horses to your ebon car!
Back to your Nile! Or if you are grown sick of dead divinities 140

Follow some roving lion's spoor across the copper-coloured
    plain,
Reach out and hale him by the mane and bid him be your
    paramour!

Couch by his side upon the grass and set your white teeth
    in his throat
And when you hear his dying note lash your long flanks of
    polished brass

And take a tiger for your mate, whose amber sides are
    flecked with black,

104

And ride upon his gilded back in triumph through the
    Theban gate,

And toy with him in amorous jests, and when he turns,
    and snarls, and gnaws,
O smite him with your jasper claws! and bruise him with
    your agate breasts!

*

Why are you tarrying? Get hence! I weary of your sullen
    ways,
I weary of your steadfast gaze, your somnolent magnificence.   150

Your horrible and heavy breath makes the light flicker in
    the lamp,
And on my brow I feel the damp and dreadful dews of night
    and death.

Your eyes are like fantastic moons that shiver in some
    stagnant lake,
Your tongue is like a scarlet snake that dances to fantastic
    tunes,

Your pulse makes poisonous melodies, and your black
    throat is like the hole
Left by some torch or burning coal on Saracenic tapestries.

Away! The sulphur-coloured stars are hurrying through
    the Western gate!
Away! Or it may be too late to climb their silent silver cars!

See, the dawn shivers round the grey gilt-dialled towers,
    and the rain
Streams down each diamonded pane and blurs with tears
    the wannish day.   160

What snake-tressed fury fresh from Hell, with uncouth
    gestures and unclean,
Stole from the poppy-drowsy queen and led you to a
    student's cell?

*

What songless tongueless ghost of sin crept through the
    curtains of the night,
And saw my taper burning bright, and knocked, and bade
    you enter in.

Are there not others more accursed, whiter with leprosies
    than I?
Are Abana and Pharphar dry that you come here to slake
    your thirst?

Get hence, you loathsome mystery! Hideous animal, get
    hence!
You wake in me each bestial sense, you make me what I
    would not be.

You make my creed a barren sham, you wake foul dreams
    of sensual life,
And Atys with his blood-stained knife were better than the
    thing I am.   170

False Sphinx! False Sphinx! By reedy Styx old Charon,
    leaning on his oar,
Waits for my coin. Go thou before, and leave me to my
    crucifix,

Whose pallid burden, sick with pain, watches the world
    with wearied eyes,
And weeps for every soul that dies, and weeps for every
    soul in vain.

The Ballad of Reading Gaol

In Memoriam C.T.W.
Sometime trooper of the Royal Horse Guards
Obiit H.M. Prison, Reading, Berkshire
7 July 1896

I

He did not wear his scarlet coat,
  For blood and wine are red,
And blood and wine were on his hands
  When they found him with the dead,
The poor dead woman whom he loved,
  And murdered in her bed.

He walked amongst the Trial Men
  In a suit of shabby gray;
A cricket cap was on his head,
  And his step seemed light and gay;   10
But I never saw a man who looked
  So wistfully at the day.

I never saw a man who looked
  With such a wistful eye
Upon that little tent of blue
  Which prisoners call the sky,
And at every drifting cloud that went
  With sails of silver by.

I walked, with other souls in pain,
  Within another ring,   20
And was wondering if the man had done
  A great or little thing,
When a voice behind me whispered low,
  'That fellow's got to swing.'

Dear Christ! the very prison walls
    Suddenly seemed to reel,
And the sky above my head became
    Like a casque of scorching steel;
And, though I was a soul in pain,
    My pain I could not feel.   30

I only knew what hunted thought
    Quickened his step, and why
He looked upon the garish day
    With such a wistful eye;
The man had killed the thing he loved,
    And so he had to die.

                    *

Yet each man kills the thing he loves,
    By each let this be heard,
Some do it with a bitter look,
    Some with a flattering word,   40
The coward does it with a kiss,
    The brave man with a sword!

Some kill their love when they are young,
    And some when they are old;
Some strangle with the hands of Lust,
    Some with the hands of Gold:
The kindest use a knife, because
    The dead so soon grow cold.

Some love too little, some too long,
    Some sell, and others buy;   50
Some do the deed with many tears,
    And some without a sigh:
For each man kills the thing he loves.
    Yet each man does not die.

He does not die a death of shame
    On a day of dark disgrace,
Nor have a noose about his neck,

108

Nor a cloth upon his face,
Nor drop feet foremost through the floor
   Into an empty space.   60

                 *

He does not sit with silent men
   Who watch him night and day;
Who watch him when he tries to weep,
   And when he tries to pray;
Who watch him lest himself should rob
   The prison of its prey.

He does not wake at dawn to see
   Dread figures throng his room,
The shivering Chaplain robed in white,
   The Sheriff stern with gloom,   70
And the Governor all in shiny black,
   With the yellow face of Doom.

He does not rise in piteous haste
   To put on convict-clothes,
While some coarse-mouthed Doctor gloats, and notes
   Each new and nerve-twitched pose,
Fingering a watch whose little ticks
   Are like horrible hammer-blows.

He does not know that sickening thirst
   That sands one's throat, before   80
The hangman with his gardener's gloves
   Slips through the padded door,
And binds one with three leathern thongs,
   That the throat may thirst no more.

He does not bend his head to hear
   The Burial Office read,
Nor, while the terror of his soul
   Tells him he is not dead,
Cross his own coffin, as he moves
   Into the hideous shed.   90

He does not stare upon the air
    Through a little roof of glass:
He does not pray with lips of clay
    For his agony to pass;
Nor feel upon his shuddering cheek
    The kiss of Caiaphas.

II

Six weeks our guardsman walked the yard,
    In the suit of shabby grey:
His cricket cap was on his head,
    And his step seemed light and gay,   100
But I never saw a man who looked
    So wistfully at the day.

I never saw a man who looked
    With such a wistful eye
Upon that little tent of blue
    Which prisoners call the sky,
And at every wandering cloud that trailed
    Its ravelled fleeces by.

He did not wring his hands, as do
    Those witless men who dare   110
To try to rear the changeling Hope
    In the cave of black Despair:
He only looked upon the sun,
    And drank the morning air.

He did not wring his hands nor weep,
    Nor did he peek or pine,
But he drank the air as though it held
    Some healthful anodyne;
With open mouth he drank the sun
    As though it had been wine!   120

And I and all the souls in pain,
    Who tramped the other ring,
Forgot if we ourselves had done

110

A great or little thing,
And watched with gaze of dull amaze
    The man who had to swing.

And strange it was to see him pass
    With a step so light and gay,
And strange it was to see him look
    So wistfully at the day,
And strange it was to think that he
    Had such a debt to pay.

                    *

For oak and elm have pleasant leaves
    That in the spring-time shoot:
But grim to see is the gallows-tree,
    With its adder-bitten root,
And, green or dry, a man must die
    Before it bears its fruit!

The loftiest place is that seat of grace
    For which all worldlings try:
But who would stand in hempen band
    Upon a scaffold high,
And through a murderer's collar take
    His last look at the sky?

It is sweet to dance to violins
    When Love and Life are fair:
To dance to flutes, to dance to lutes
    Is delicate and rare:
But it is not sweet with nimble feet
    To dance upon the air!

So with curious eyes and sick surmise
    We watched him day by day,
And wondered if each one of us
    Would end the self-same way,
For none can tell to what red Hell
    His sightless soul may stray.

At last the dead man walked no more
    Amongst the Trial Men,
And I knew that he was standing up
    In the black dock's dreadful pen,   160
And that never would I see his face
    In God's sweet world again.

Like two doomed ships that pass in storm
    We had crossed each other's way:
But we made no sign, we said no word,
    We had no word to say;
For we did not meet in the holy night,
    But in the shameful day.

A prison wall was round us both,
    Two outcast men we were: 170
The world had thrust us from its heart,
    And God from out His care:
And the iron gin that waits for Sin
    Had caught us in its snare.

III

In Debtors' Yard the stones are hard,
    And the dripping wall is high,
So it was there he took the air
    Beneath the leaden sky,
And by each side a Warder walked,
    For fear the man might die.   180

Or else he sat with those who watched
    His anguish night and day;
Who watched him when he rose to weep,
    And when he crouched to pray;
Who watched him lest himself should rob
    Their scaffold of its prey.

The Governor was strong upon
    The Regulations Act:
The Doctor said that Death was but

A scientific fact: 190
And twice a day the Chaplain called,
    And left a little tract.

And twice a day he smoked his pipe,
    And drank his quart of beer:
His soul was resolute, and held
    No hiding-place for fear;
He often said that he was glad
    The hangman's hands were near.

But why he said so strange a thing
    No Warder dared to ask: 200
For he to whom a watcher's doom
    Is given as his task,
Must set a lock upon his lips,
    And make his face a mask.

Or else he might be moved, and try
    To comfort or console:
And what should Human Pity do
    Pent up in Murderers' Hole?
What word of grace in such a place
    Could help a brother's soul?   210

*

With slouch and swing around the ring
    We trod the Fools' Parade!
We did not care: we knew we were
    The Devil's Own Brigade:
And shaven head and feet of lead
    Make a merry masquerade.

We tore the tarry rope to shreds
    With blunt and bleeding nails;
We rubbed the doors, and scrubbed the floors,
    And cleaned the shining rails: 220
And, rank by rank, we soaped the plank,
    And clattered with the pails.

113

We sewed the sacks, we broke the stones,
    We turned the dusty drill:
We banged the tins, and bawled the hymns,
    And sweated on the mill:
But in the heart of every man
    Terror was lying still.

So still it lay that every day
    Crawled like a weed-clogged wave: 230
And we forgot the bitter lot
    That waits for fool and knave,
Till once, as we tramped in from work,
    We passed an open grave.

With yawning mouth the yellow hole
    Gaped for a living thing;
The very mud cried out for blood
    To the thirsty asphalte ring:
And we knew that ere one dawn grew fair
    Some prisoner had to swing. 240

Right in we went, with soul intent
    On Death and Dread and Doom:
The hangman, with his little bag,
    Went shuffling through the gloom:
And each man trembled as he crept
    Into his numbered tomb.

*

That night the empty corridors
    Were full of forms of Fear,
And up and down the iron town
    Stole feet we could not hear, 250
And through the bars that hide the stars
    White faces seemed to peer.

He lay as one who lies and dreams
    In a pleasant meadow-land,
The watchers watched him as he slept,

114

And could not understand
How one could sleep so sweet a sleep
　　With a hangman close at hand.

But there is no sleep when men must weep
　　Who never yet have wept:　　　　　　　　　　260
So we – the fool, the fraud, the knave –
　　That endless vigil kept,
And through each brain on hands of pain
　　Another's terror crept.

Alas! it is a fearful thing
　　To feel another's guilt!
For, right within, the sword of Sin
　　Pierced to its poisoned hilt,
And as molten lead were the tears we shed
　　For the blood we had not spilt.　　　　　　　270

The Warders with their shoes of felt
　　Crept by each padlocked door,
And peeped and saw, with eyes of awe,
　　Grey figures on the floor,
And wondered why men knelt to pray
　　Who never prayed before.

All through the night we knelt and prayed,
　　Mad mourners of a corse!
The troubled plumes of midnight were
　　The plumes upon a hearse:　　　　　　　　　280
And bitter wine upon a sponge
　　Was the savour of Remorse.

*

The grey cock crew, the red cock crew,
　　But never came the day:
And croooked shapes of Terror crouched,
　　In the corners where we lay:
And each evil sprite that walks by night
　　Before us seemed to play.

115

They glided past, they glided fast,
　　Like travellers through a mist:　　　　　　　　290
They mocked the moon in a rigadoon
　　Of delicate turn and twist,
And with formal pace and loathsome grace
　　The phantoms kept their tryst.

With mop and mow, we saw them go,
　　Slim shadows hand in hand:
About, about, in ghostly rout
　　They trod a saraband:
And the damned grotesques made arabesques,
　　Like the wind upon the sand!　　　　　　　　300

With the pirouettes of marionettes,
　　They tripped on pointed tread:
But with flutes of Fear they filled the ear,
　　As their grisly masque they led,
And loud they sang, and long they sang,
　　For they sang to wake the dead.

'Oho!' they cried, 'The world is wide,
　　But fettered limbs go lame!
And once, or twice, to throw the dice
　　Is a gentlemanly game,　　　　　　　　310
But he does not win who plays with Sin
　　In the secret House of Shame.'

No things of air these antics were,
　　That frolicked with such glee:
To men whose lives were held in gyves,
　　And whose feet might not go free,
Ah! wounds of Christ! they were living things,
　　Most terrible to see.

Around, around, they waltzed and wound;
　　Some wheeled in smirking pairs;　　　　　　320
With the mincing step of a demirep

116

Some sidled up the stairs:
And with subtle sneer, and fawning leer,
   Each helped us at our prayers.

The morning wind began to moan,
   But still the night went on:
Through its giant loom the web of gloom
   Crept till each thread was spun:
And, as we prayed, we grew afraid
   Of the Justice of the Sun.   330

The moaning wind went wandering round
   The weeping prison-wall:
Till like a wheel of turning steel
   We felt the minutes crawl:
O moaning wind! what had we done
   To have such a seneschal?

At last I saw the shadowed bars,
   Like a lattice wrought in lead,
Move right across the whitewashed wall
   That faced by three-plank bed,   340
And I knew that somewhere in the world
   God's dreadful dawn was red.

At six o'clock we cleaned our cells,
   At seven all was still,
But the sough and swing of a mighty wing
   The prison seemed to fill,
For the Lord of Death with icy breath
   Had entered in to kill.

He did not pass in purple pomp,
   Nor ride a moon-white steed.   350
Three yards of cord and a sliding board
   Are all the gallows' need:
So with rope of shame the Herald came
   To do the secret deed.

We were as men who through a fen
  Of filthy darkness grope:
We did not dare to breathe a prayer,
  Or to give our anguish scope:
Something was dead in each of us,
  And what was dead was Hope.   360

For Man's grim Justice goes its way,
  And will not swerve aside:
It slays the weak, it slays the strong,
  It has a deadly stride:
With iron heel it slays the strong,
  The monstrous parricide!

We waited for the stroke of eight:
  Each tongue was thick with thirst:
For the stroke of eight is the stroke of Fate
  That makes a man accursed,   370
And Fate will use a running noose
  For the best man and the worst.

We had no other thing to do,
  Save to wait for the sign to come:
So, like things of stone in a valley lone,
  Quiet we sat and dumb:
But each man's heart beat thick and quick,
  Like a madman on a drum!

With sudden shock the prison-clock
  Smote on the shivering air,   380
And from all the gaol rose up a wail
  Of impotent despair,
Like the sound that frightened marshes hear
  From some leper in his lair.

And as one sees most fearful things
  In the crystal of a dream,
We saw the greasy hempen rope

118

Hooked to the blackened beam,
And heard the prayer the hangman's snare
   Strangled into a scream.   390

And all the woe that moved him so
   That he gave that bitter cry,
And the wild regrets, and the bloody sweats,
   None knew so well as I:
For he who lives more lives than one
   More deaths than one must die.

IV

There is no chapel on the day
   On which they hang a man:
The Chaplain's heart is far too sick,
   Or his face is far too wan,   400
Or there is that written in his eyes
   Which none should look upon.

So they kept us close till nigh on noon,
   And then they rang the bell,
And the Warders with their jangling keys
   Opened each listening cell,
And down the iron stair we tramped,
   Each from his separate Hell.

Out into God's sweet air we went,
   But not in wonted way,   410
For this man's face was white with fear,
   And that man's face was grey,
And I never saw sad men who looked
   So wistfully at the day.

I never saw sad men who looked
   With such a wistful eye
Upon that little tent of blue
   We prisoners call the sky,
And at every careless cloud that passed
   In happy freedom by.   420

But there were those amongst us all
    Who walked with downcast head,
And knew that, had each got his due,
    They should have died instead:
He had but killed a thing that lived,
    Whilst they had killed the dead.

For he who sins a second time
    Wakes a dead soul to pain,
And draws it from its spotted shroud,
    And makes it bleed again,   430
And makes it bleed great gouts of blood,
    And makes it bleed in vain!

                    *

Like ape or clown, in monstrous garb
    With crooked arrows starred,
Silently we went round and round,
    The slippery asphalte yard;
Silently we went round and round
    And no man spoke a word.

Silently we went round and round,
    And through each hollow mind   440
The Memory of dreadful things
    Rushed like a dreadful wind,
And Horror stalked before each man,
    And Terror crept behind.

                    *

The Warders strutted up and down,
    And kept their herd of brutes,
Their uniforms were spick and span,
    And they wore their Sunday suits,
But we knew the work they had been at,
    By the quicklime on their boots.   450

For where a grave had opened wide,
    There was no grave at all:
Only a stretch of mud and sand

By the hideous prison-wall,
And a little heap of burning lime,
    That the man should have his pall.

For he has a pall, this wretched man,
    Such as few men can claim:
Deep down below a prison-yard,
    Naked for greater shame,
He lies, with fetters on each foot,
    Wrapt in a sheet of flame!

And all the while the burning lime
    Eats flesh and bone away,
It eats the brittle bone by night,
    And the soft flesh by day,
It eats the flesh and bone by turns,
    But it eats the heart alway.

                    *

For three long years they will not sow
    Or root or seedling there:
For three long years the unblessed spot
    Will sterile be and bare,
And look upon the wondering sky
    With unreproachful stare.

They think a murderer's heart would taint
    Each simple seed they sow.
It is not true! God's kindly earth
    Is kindlier than men know,
And the red rose would but blow more red,
    The white rose whiter blow.

Out of his mouth a red, red rose!
    Out of his heart a white!
For who can say by what strange way,
    Christ brings His will to light,
Since the barren staff the pilgrim bore
    Bloomed in the great Pope's sight?

460

470

480

But neither milk-white rose nor red
    May bloom in prison air;
The shard, the pebble, and the flint,
    Are what they give us there:
For flowers have been known to heal
    A common man's despair.

So never will wine-red rose or white,
    Petal by petal, fall
On that stretch of mud and sand that lies
    By the hideous prison-wall,
To tell the men who tramp the yard
    That God's Son died for all.

*

Yet though the hideous prison-wall
    Still hems him round and round,
And a spirit may not walk by night
    That is with fetters bound,
And a spirit may but weep that lies
    In such unholy ground,

He is at peace – this wretched man –
    At peace, or will be soon:
There is no thing to make him mad,
    Nor does Terror walk at noon,
For the lampless Earth in which he lies
    Has neither Sun nor Moon.

They hanged him as a beast is hanged:
    They did not even toll
A requiem that might have brought
    Rest to his startled soul,
But hurriedly they took him out,
    And hid him in a hole.

They stripped him of his canvas clothes,
    And gave him to the flies:
They mocked the swollen purple throat,

490

500

510

And the stark and staring eyes: 520
And with laughter loud they heaped the shroud
   In which their convict lies.

The Chaplain would not kneel to pray
   By his dishonoured grave:
Nor mark it with that blessed Cross
   That Christ for sinners gave,
Because the man was one of those
   Whom Christ came down to save.

Yet all is well; he has but passed
   To life's appointed bourne: 530
And alien tears will fill for him
   Pity's long-broken urn,
For his mourners will be outcast men,
   And outcasts always mourn.

V

I know not whether Laws be right,
   Or whether Laws be wrong;
All that we know who lie in gaol
   Is that the wall is strong;
And that each day is like a year,
   A year whose days are long.   540

But this I know, that every Law
   That men have made for Man,
Since first Man took his brother's life,
   And the sad world began,
But straws the wheat and saves the chaff
   With a most evil fan.

This too I know – and wise it were
   If each could know the same –
That every prison that men build
   Is built with bricks of shame,   550
And bound with bars lest Christ should see
   How men their brothers maim.

With bars they blur the gracious moon,
    And blind the goodly sun:
And they do well to hide their Hell,
    For in it things are done
That Son of God nor son of Man
    Ever should look upon!

*

The vilest deeds like poison weeds,
    Bloom well in prison-air;   560
It is only what is good in Man
    That wastes and withers there:
Pale Anguish keeps the heavy gate,
    And the Warder is Despair.

For they starve the little frightened child
    Till it weeps both night and day:
And they scourge the weak, and flog the fool,
    And gibe the old and grey,
And some grow mad, and all grow bad,
    And none a word may say.   570

Each narrow cell in which we dwell
    Is a foul and dark latrine,
And the fetid breath of living Death
    Chokes up each grated screen,
And all, but Lust, is turned to dust
    In Humanity's machine.

The brackish water that we drink
    Creeps with a loathsome slime,
And the bitter bread they weigh in scales
    Is full of chalk and lime,   580
And Sleep will not lie down, but walks
    Wild-eyed, and cries to Time.

*

But though lean Hunger and green Thirst
    Like asp with adder fight,
We have little care of prison fare,

For what chills and kills outright
Is that every stone one lifts by day
  Becomes one's heart by night.

With midnight always in one's heart,
  And twilight in one's cell,   590
We turn the crank, or tear the rope,
  Each in his separate Hell,
And the silence is more awful far
  Than the sound of a brazen bell.

And never a human voice comes near
  To speak a gentle word:
And the eye that watches through the door
  Is pitiless and hard:
And by all forgot, we rot and rot,
  With soul and body marred.   600

And thus we rust Life's iron chain
  Degraded and alone:
And some men curse, and some men weep,
  And some men make no moan:
But God's eternal Laws are kind
  And break the heart of stone.

*

And every human heart that breaks,
  In prison-cell or yard,
Is as that broken box that gave
  Its treasure to the Lord,   610
And filled the unclean leper's house
  With the scent of costliest nard.

Ah! happy they whose hearts can break
  And peace of pardon win!
How else may man make straight his plan
  And cleanse his soul from Sin?
How else but through a broken heart
  May Lord Christ enter in?   620

And he of the swollen purple throat,
    And the stark and staring eyes,
Waits for the holy hands that took
    The Thief to Paradise;
And a broken and a contrite heart
    The Lord will not despise.

The man in red who reads the Law
    Gave him three weeks of life,
Three little weeks in which to heal
    His soul of his soul's strife,   630
And cleanse from every blot of blood
    The hand that held the knife.

And with tears of blood he cleansed the hand,
    The hand that held the steel:
For only blood can wipe out blood,
    And only tears can heal:
And the crimson stain that was of Cain
    Became Christ's snow-white seal.

VI

In Reading gaol by Reading town
    There is a pit of shame,   640
And in it lies a wretched man
    Eaten by teeth of flame,
In a burning winding-sheet he lies,
    And his grave has got no name.

And there, till Christ call forth the dead,
    In silence let him lie:
No need to waste the foolish tear,
    Or heave the windy sigh:
The man had killed the thing he loved,
    And so he had to die.   650

And all men kill the thing they love,
    By all let this be heard,
Some do it with a bitter look,
    Some with a flattering word,
The coward does it with a kiss,
    The brave man with a sword!

Notes

To attempt to document the wealth of reference and allusion in Wilde's poetry would result in a pedantic clutter at odds with the spirit of the reading experience. What follows are a few points of elucidation which might prove helpful.

19   *'Hélas!'* (Alas): introductory sonnet to the first and subsequent editions, not included in the list of contents which it preceded. The poem is discussed in Ellmann, *Oscar Wilde*, pp.132-4.

19   *'Ave Imperatrix'* – 'Hail, Commanding Mistress', with 'A Poem on England' originally included in the title.

33   *'Requiescat'*: said to have been written in memory of Wilde's little sister, Isola, who died 23 February 1867, aged eight.

34   'The Burden of Itys': Itys, in Greek mythology, was the son of Procne, whom she killed and served up to her husband, Tereus, in revenge for his violation and silencing (by cutting out her tongue) of her sister Philomela. As Tereus tried to slay the sisters the three of them were transformed into birds. The speaker of the poem loosely takes on the character of Itys. 1.12, *in partibus* – in foreign parts, abroad.

47 'Charmides': Wilde said 'Charmides' was his 'favourite poem. I think it is my best. It is the most perfect and finished.' The story is elaborated out of an anecdote related in one of the dialogues of Lucian (*c.*115-*c.*200).

70 'Camma': Apparently written to Ellen Terry when she played the part of Camma in Tennyson's play, *The Cup* early in 1881.

77 *'Impression, Le Réveillon'*: Wilde's poem describes dawn after spending the night at *un réveillon* (a midnight supper, especially at Christmas Eve or New Year's Eve).

77 *'Quia Multum Amavi'* – Because I have loved much.

82 'ΓΛΥΚΥΠΙΚΡΟΣ ΕΡΩΣ' – Sweetly Bitter Love. This title is taken from Sappho. See, variously, inc. no.40 of *Poetae Lyrici Graeci*: ed. Theodor Bergk (1843; subsequent edns. 1878-82, etc.) The second (English) title is from the 1882 edition.

85 'The Harlot's House': first published 1885.

88 'To My Wife, with a copy of my poems': first appeared in 1893.

88 'To L.L.': L.L. is Lillie Langtry, with whom Wilde might have had an affair in the late 1870s. See Ellmann, *Oscar Wilde*, pp.107-8. The poem was written in 1884 and first published in the first collected edition of 1908. A shorter draft, entitled 'Roses and Rue', had appeared in 'Midsummer Dreams', the Summer number of *Society* (June, 1885).

93 'Chorus of Cloud Maidens': translated from the *Clouds* of Aristophanes. ΣΤΡΟΦΗ – Strophe.

94 ΘΡΗΝΩΙΔΙΑ – A Song of Lamentation, translated from the *Hecuba* of Euripides. ΑΝΤΙΣΤΡΟΦΗ – Antistrophe.

95 *The Sphinx*: first published in 1894 in extravagant book form.

129 *The Ballad of Reading Gaol*: first published 1898 in book form. Six editions were called for within the year; the seventh and last of the authorised editions appearing in June 1899.